MW01713766

QUILTING

The Complete Stage by Stage Guide to Master the Art of Sewing a Quilt in no time; with Sewing Patterns, Awesome Projects with Pictures.

Deborah Collins

Table of contents

CHAPTER ONE

INTRODUCTION TO QUILTING

A lot of persons have always wanted to make beautiful quilting work. Some think you must have lots of sewing experiences before you can attempt quilting. So many questions on your minds on how best to quilt as a beginner, don't you worry in here you will find the answers you seek.

Quilting is a part of sewing that a few of us love to stall out into occasionally (or, for other people, constantly), for the sheer love of sewing and getting completely lost to the world in finicky small details... and there's no more prominent rush than a completed item that closely resembles loving time was spent on it. It's one of the keenest and liberal endowments you can give and stories can be told in the stitches. For those of you who have been peering toward your crude sacks loaded with small amounts of excellent materials: what better approach to gather each one of those recollections in a single spot than by scrap-busting with your first quilt?!

Likewise, you're genuine inventive flare may not generally go down well when applied to a thing of dress yet on a blanket, hell... if need be, anything goes! Thus, in light of this current, it's the ideal opportunity for some quilting lessons for beginners... a quilting 101.

Beginner Quilting

Right off the bat, there's no compelling reason to go out and get some very expensive machine in light of the fact that your residential sewing machine will work, if you know the what's and wherefores and you don't mean to cover a church building wall with your enormous and many-sided quilt.

So YES, Yes you can do quilting utilizing a residential or domestic sewing machine!

When sewing on a residential machine, it's ideal to utilize a walking foot. Obviously, as you develop your skills and take on greater and greater activities, it is incredible to put resources into an extravagant dancy Bernina 880 with the free arm — I'm a colossal enthusiast of Bernina as you most likely know–however you positively don't have to begin there. When utilizing your local sewing machine, make sure to keep the two sides of the blanket moved up and cut to spare space and inconvenience.

The fundamental or basic quilt is developed in three layers: the backing, the batting, and the quilt top. The last is the part into which a large portion of your difficult work will have gone, all that piecing and designing, such consideration and making. Obviously, what material you utilize, that is all up to you, albeit generally quilts were all-cotton.

Actually, in case you're a learner I would prescribe adhering to cotton all through (also advice you use cotton thread) in light of the fact that you'll discover the layers don't slip and slide so a lot, making them a lot simpler to work with. Silks and Polyesters will tend to slide and in case you're simply beginning, you probably won't be in the state of mind for such dissatisfactions!

CHAPTER TWO

STEP BY STEP GUIDELINES TO SEW A QUILT!

How to Sew a Quilt! (Quilting 101)

My biggest passion as long as craft work is concerned is quilting. I feel it's probably hereditary.

I likewise believe it's an ability that is valuable amazing... quilts are delightful and practical and I believe them to be the best blessing on the planet. (Truly, who wouldn't need a quilt?) They're family treasures, went down through the ages until they self-destruct. They're an astounding method to make use of scrap material, and an easy first sewing venture.

Also I discover sewing/cutting them extremely restorative... loads of straight lines with no weight or pressure. :)

In this book I'm going to take you through making a fundamental queen size 9-fix patchwork quilt. These are my top picks since they are not confounded and can be finished in far less time than other quilt sorts.

I'll train you about the apparatuses required for quilting, how to cut squares, selecting fabrics or materials, batting, making a quilt sandwich, how to pick and append support, and collecting the quilt top in addition to other things. It's likewise critical to take note of that you can without much of a stretch total one of these in two or three weeks - I began this one on February seventh, and completed it on March third - yet that incorporated heaps of documentation and just working making use of daylight. ;)

I strongly believe that this book will be very useful for you and motivates you to knit.

Sincerely, I believe we do need more quilts in this world.

Below I will be showing you 33 stages on how you can successfully sew a quilt from start to finish, whether as a beginner or a pro.

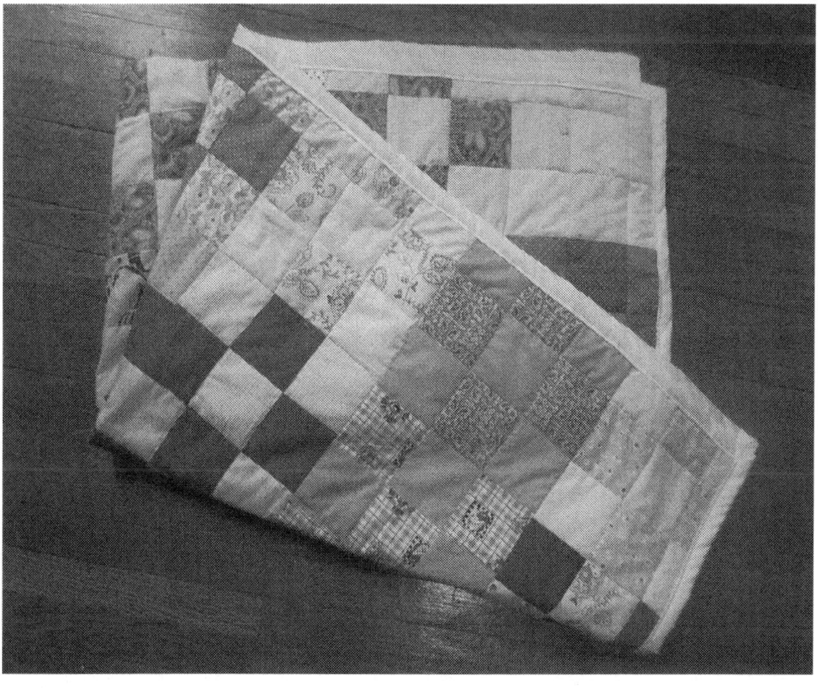

Stage 1: Fundamental Quilting Definitions

Like most abilities, quilting accompanies its own dialect. I thought I'd include this here and give my own meanings of huge numbers of the words I'll be utilizing in this project.

Backing or Support: the base piece of the quilt, regularly made of one strong bit of material. Most occasions this material is white - I like to utilize sheets for this!

Batting: the comfortable center of a quilt - can be produced using cotton, polyester or wool. Normally purchased by the size of the quilt you're making - found in rolls.

Bias- tape: segments of material used to tie the edges of a quilt.

Binding: the edging of a quilt - it encases the crude edges.

Blocks: a bit of material produced using sewing 9 squares together.

Piecing: sewing together bits of material to frame the top layer of the quilt, regularly done in squares.

Quilt sandwich: this is what is known as the three layers. They are; top, batting and backing.

Quilt top: pieced material commonly set up in squares.

Quilting: sewing through numerous layers of material to make one thick layer - regularly includes three sections: fabric top, batting center, material base.

Seam allowance: 1/4 inch is the standard seam allowance for quilting

Square: smaller bits of material that are sewn together to make a bigger, square bit of material. For this situation, we will sew together 9 little squares to make one huge square. A quilt top is comprised of these squares sewn together.

Stage 2: Tools for Quilting.

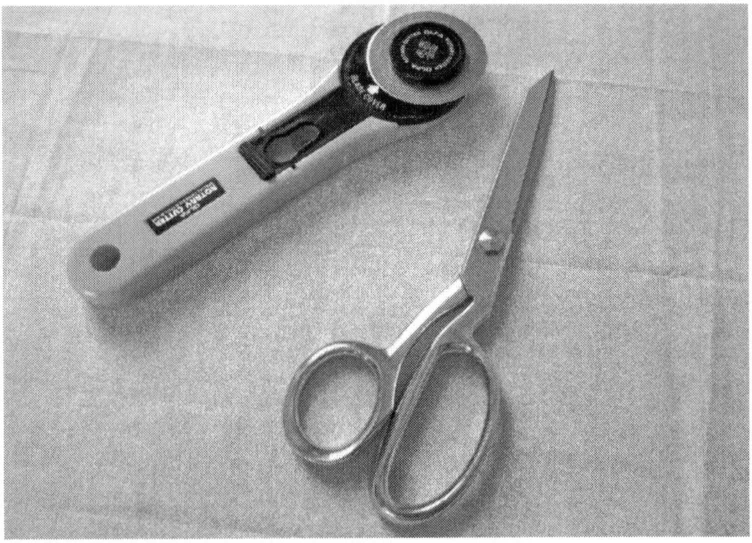

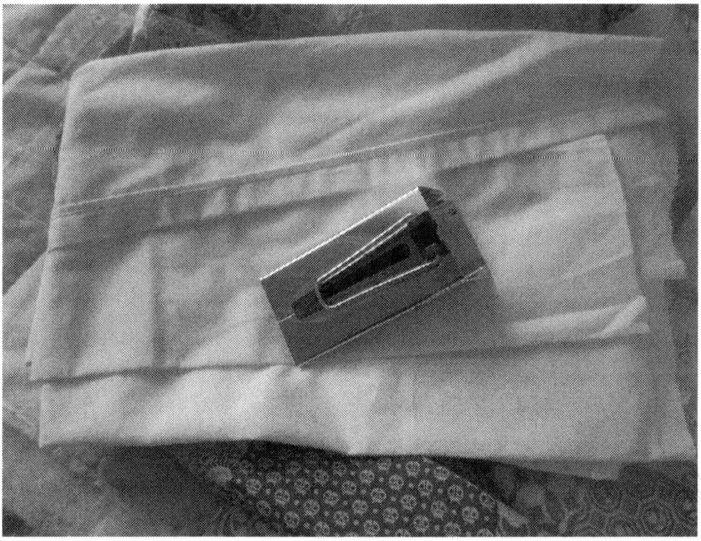

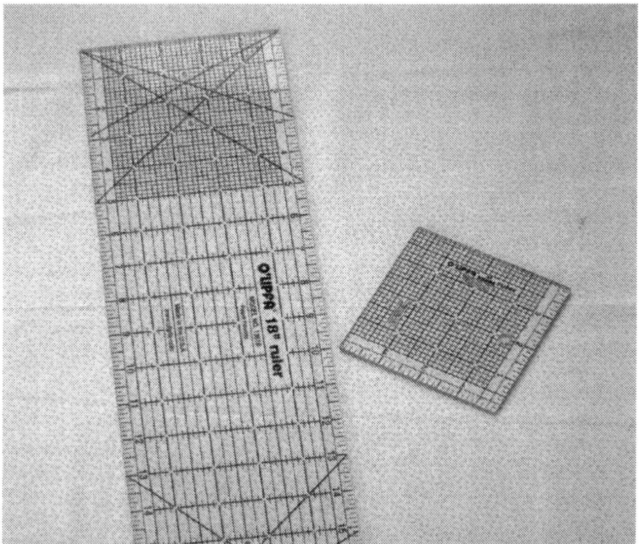
OLIPFA 18" ruler

These are a portion of the things you'll require:

- Rotary shaper and tangle + sharp scissors
- Clear rulers (ideally 5x18 inches and a 4x4 inch one.)
- Bias tape creator or instant bias tape
- Clear nylon string
- White cotton string (or a polyester/cotton blend)
- 100% cotton material
- Long pins
- An iron + pressing board
- Batting
- seam ripper
- Something to use as a string garbage container (I like mason containers)

- walking foot for the machine (more clarification in stage 22)

Stage 3: A Perfect Setup.

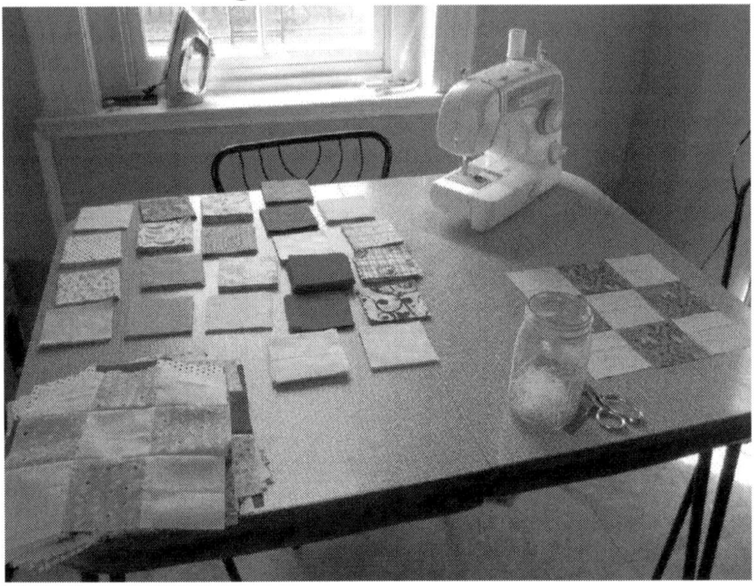

So as to do the entirety of this easily, it's ideal to have a biiiiiiig table. In the event that you don't have one of those, you can pull out the pressing board and use it as a surface, utilize additional seats, and so forth.

I like to have the option to see the entirety of my pre-cut squares when I'm working since I don't pick formats before I begin sewing, I simply make it up as I come. It's additionally significant that you can lay your unsown square format close to the sewing machine; it'll shield you from getting yourself confounded or confused.

Now, it's additionally a smart thought to make yourself a little trashcan - I utilize old mason containers for string clippings. I keep it on the contrary side of my machine and drop them in at whatever point I cut something off. I likewise attempt to keep a test square of material (in the event that the pressure on the machine goes amusing), a seam ripper, and a decent pair of scissors as close as could reasonably be expected. It'll make your life simpler.

Stage 4: Frame of a 9 Square Quilt.

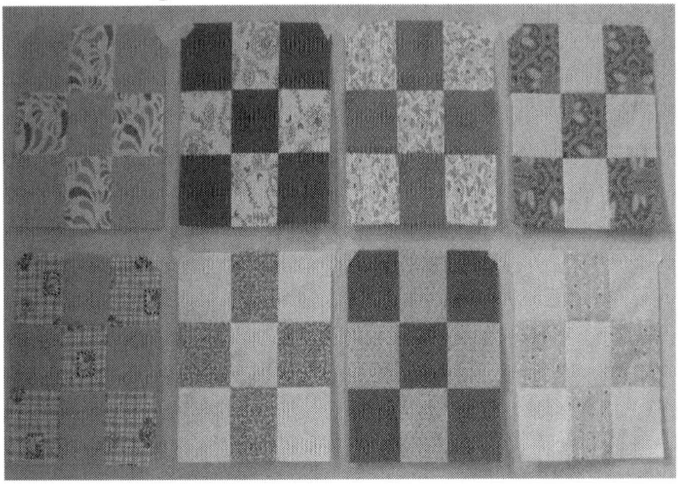

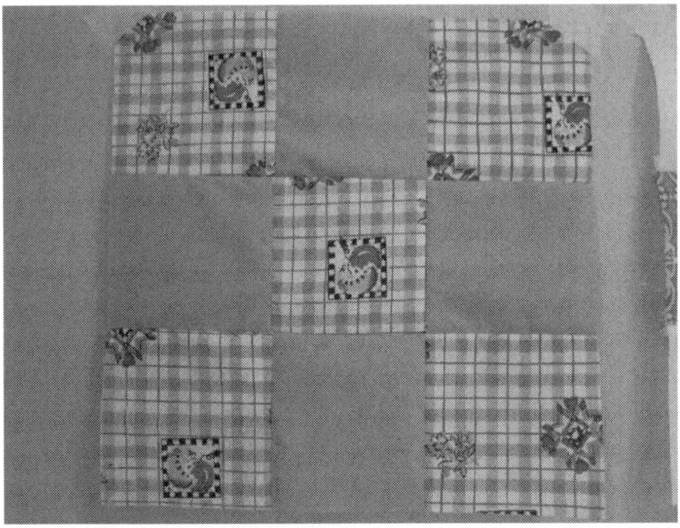

The 9 square quilts is the most classical type of quilt and is known as the queen size. This implies it is 6 squares wide and 8 squares in length.

Each square is comprised of nine squares of differentiating material - these squares are cut at 4x4inches. (So they will be 3.5x3.5 when sewn - implying that the block made out of them will be 10.5 inches square.)

You can make a wide range of structures utilizing the 9 square strategy - it relies upon colors and position. You can make a piece quilt that incorporates a wide range of material - these are my undisputed top choice. You can likewise utilize 2 colors all through a whole quilt. Or then again you can wander away from designed squares inside and out and make 8-piece characters, landscapes, and words.

Above are a few instances of various quilt squares.

Stage 5: Fabric – What Material to Purchase, How to Select.

For the basis of this quilt, the best material you can pick will be 100% cotton. Most art, material and interest stores have an area essentially marked "quilting cottons". In case you desire to do a scrap quilt, I suggest burrowing through leftover canisters and chasing around your home for garments to deconstruct and cut into squares. I did almost no looking for this quilt - the materials are a blend of my grandma's and mine. :)

In case you need to utilize two colors or accomplish something increasingly terrific, you'll have to do a little math to make sense of how much material to purchase... here are a few figures to kick you off!

Number of squares and squares in a queen size quilt:

Squares: 48 (10.5 in square sewn size)

Squares: 432 (3.5 in square sewn size)

In case you're completing 2 colors, you'll need 216 of each shade in the quilt.

Number of squares you can escape ONE YARD of material (this is expecting you've cut off the selvedge closes and are left with material 40 inches wide):

90 squares (since your material will be 36x40 inches)

I figure you all ought to have the option to make sense of the remaining based on those

- yet on the off chance that you need any extra assistance, don't be reluctant to inquire!

Stage 6: Selecting Batting.

Batting is significant in a quilt - the sort you pick will change the look, feel and warmth of your quilt.

There are three significant kinds of batting:

- Cotton (bamboo additionally falls into this class)
- Polyester

- Wool

Cotton is my undisputed top choice - it lays compliment, sews simpler and is extremely breathable. It washes well and makes for an exceptionally dependable and low upkeep quilt.

Polyester is heavier and accordingly hotter - however it tends to bundle and furthermore push its way through the quilt top after some time. (it's smarter to utilize it on light colord quilts - on darker ones, you'll see minimal white filaments jabbing through!) It is less expensive than cotton by and large.

Wool is overwhelming and retains dampness. This is best for a quilt you'll utilize principally in winter or while outdoors - wool can be kind of fastidious with regards to washing however... so read the entire package and be cautious! Shrinkage is anguishing after such work!

Batting comes in abounds in numerous sizes - from crib to ruler! It is extremely simple to get a size to suit your necessities. :)

Stage 7: Choosing Your Backing Material.

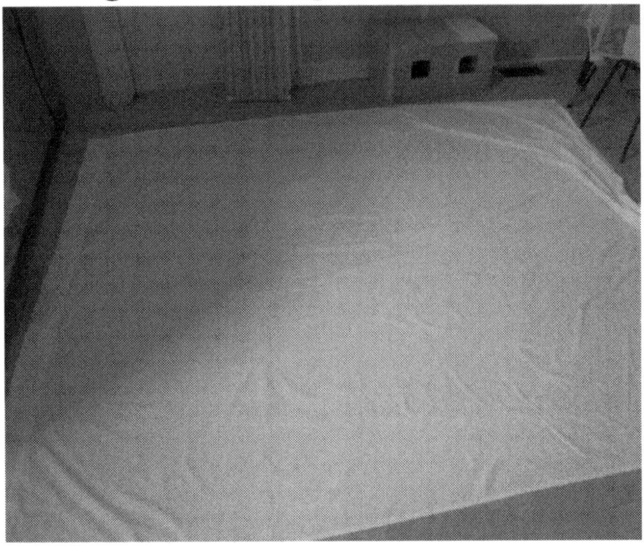

This is sufficiently straightforward - purchase a level sheet of a similar size! I truly don't do whatever else. :)

The best places to look are second hand shops or leeway racks in stores like Target. You would prefer not to spend more than $15 on it.

The shading is additionally up to you - I quite often prefer white backing since it's conventional, however on the off chance that you need the backing to align with the quilt,

go for the one you most desire.

Stage 8: Cutting Your Desired Squares.

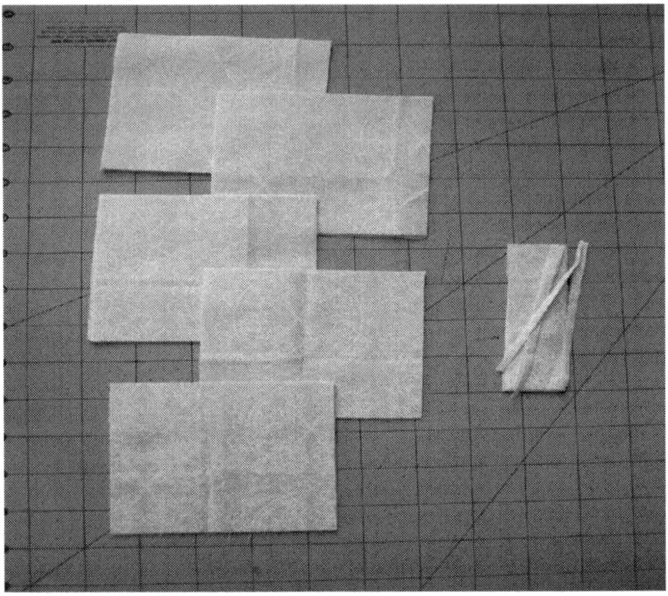

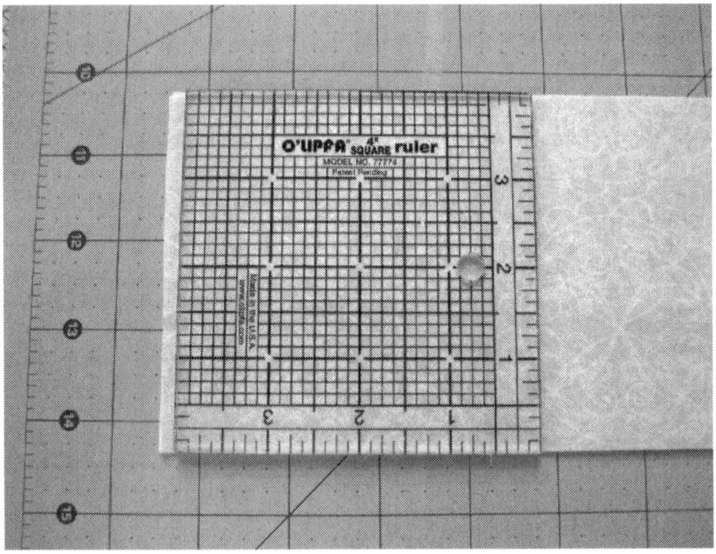

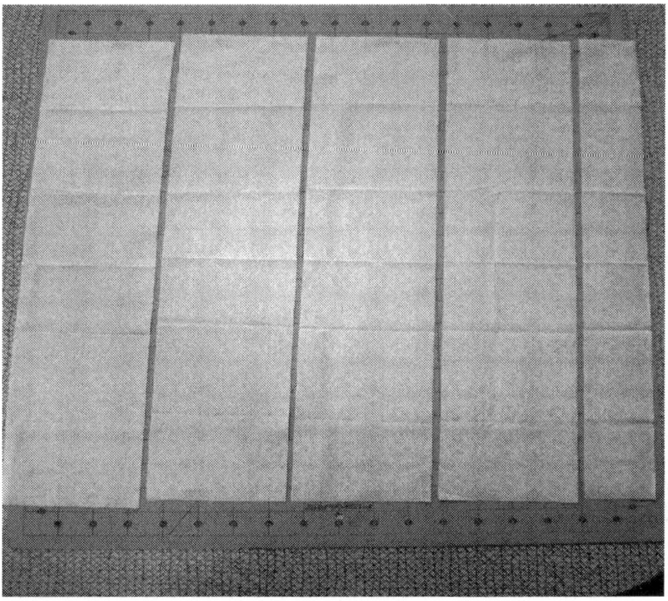

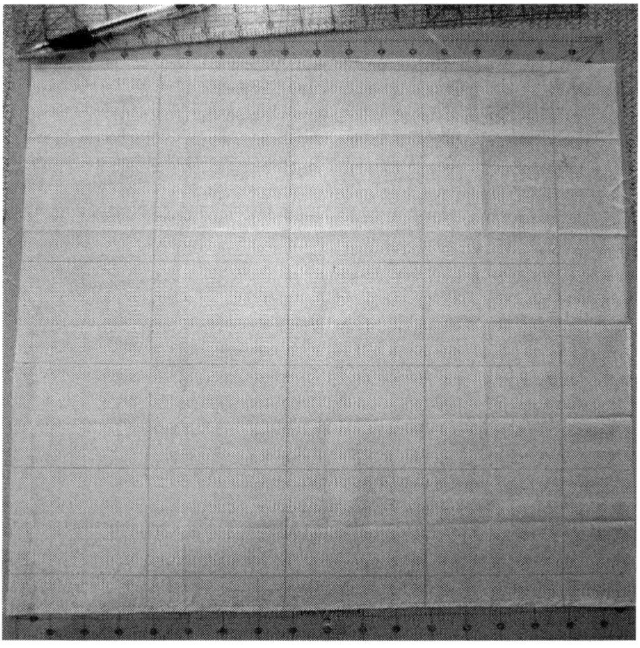

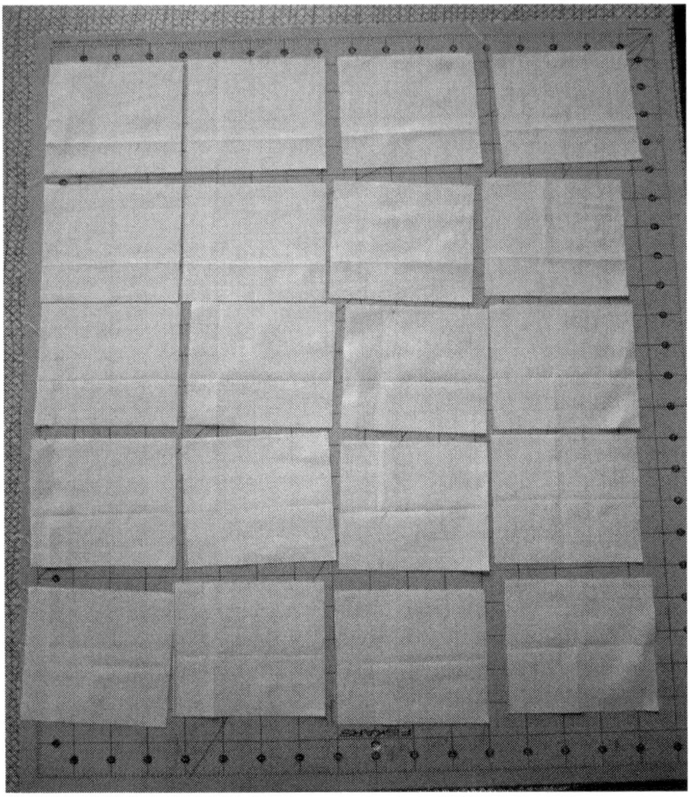

IMPORTANT: If your material is extremely wrinkly, you'll need to press it before hand for progressively accurate cutting. Try not to stress over pre-washing it - I've never done it and every one of my quilts have turned out fine and dandy.

By rotary shaper or cutter:

I utilize a rotating shaper, a cutting mat, a plain 5x18in ruler and a reasonable 4x4in ruler for this. It's a lot speedier and simpler on your hands when you're cutting a huge amount of material. Also, on the off chance that you have another cutting edge, you can without much of a stretch slice through 4 layers of material at once. :)

The most effortless approach to do this is to cut a piece of material four inches in length and afterward cut that into four inch squares. Just stress over fixing the left edge of the material - the lopsided tops and bottoms of the material can be cut off when you cut the strip into squares.

By scissors:

On the off chance that you don't possess a rotary shaper, I locate the most effortless approach to slice the squares is to draw a grid on the rear of the material. Do the four inch strips, and afterward partition them into

4 inch squares. At that point you can cut the material into pieces. You can utilize pinking shears on the off chance that you like, yet I will in general utilize customary dressmaker's shears since it goes faster.

I regularly cut a bit of material into squares and afterward check and stack those squares and proceed onward to the following bit of material. I find that it's simpler to cut all that I have into squares and afterward begin contemplating what shading mixes would glance pleasant in a square.

For whatever length of time that you can get at least four squares out of any bit of material, you can utilize it in a square!

In the following Stage we'll discuss shading blends. :)

Stage 9: Making your Pattern and Color Combinations for Blocks.

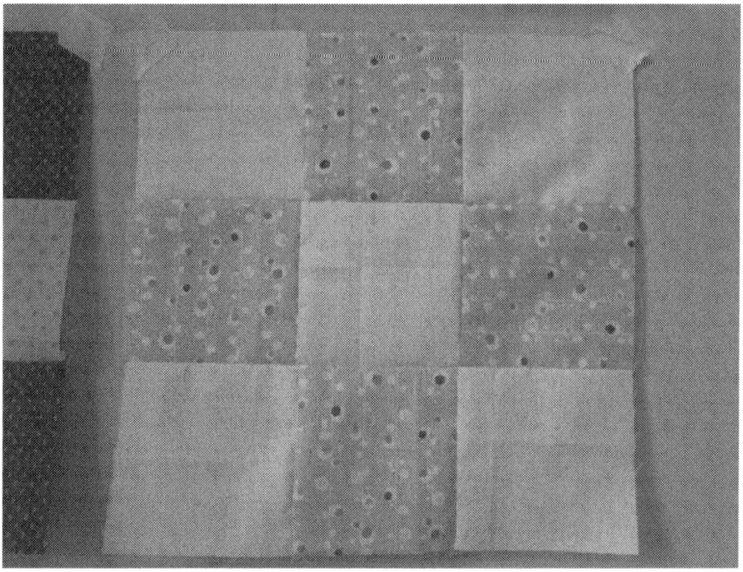

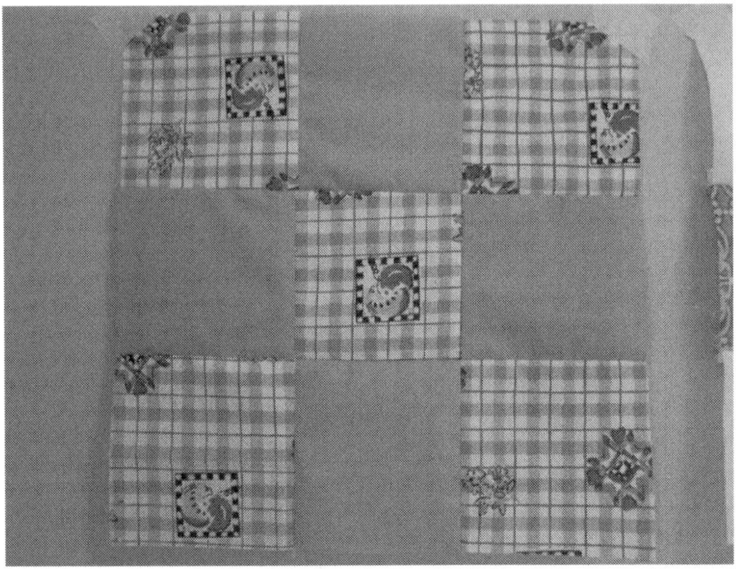

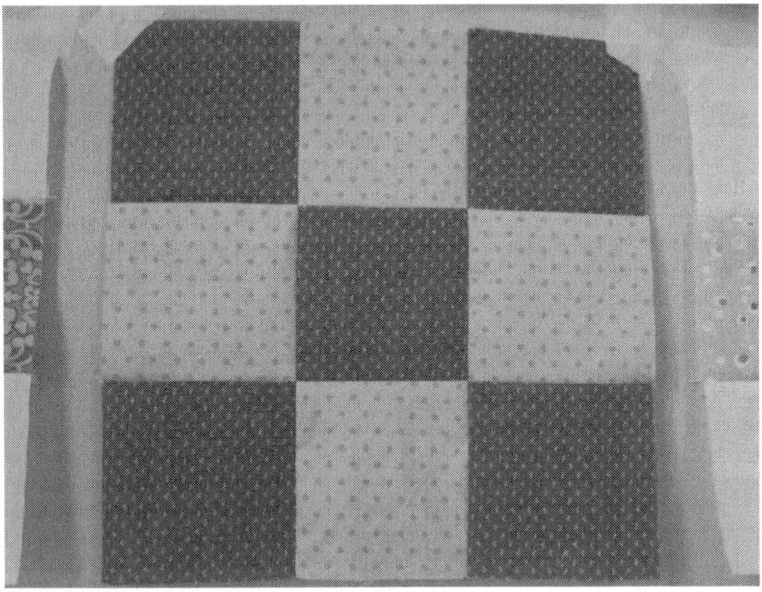

When you've cut a huge amount of squares, it's a decent an ideal opportunity to begin contemplating what goes with what. :)

Remember that each square has 4 of one color shading and 5 of another. Here are a few plans to make you go similarly as shading mixes go:

- 2 differentiating solids (like yellow and purple, blue and orange, and so forth.)
- One solid and one pattern
- One pattern and one solid that completely match with one of the colors available in the pattern
- Two particular pattern (spots and stripes, two specks of various colors, florals and checks, and so on.)

More than anything, I think that it's convenient to ensure I have pretty much equivalent measure of solids and patterns when I experience my material stash.

Stage 10: Assembling and Sewing the Squares into a Block.

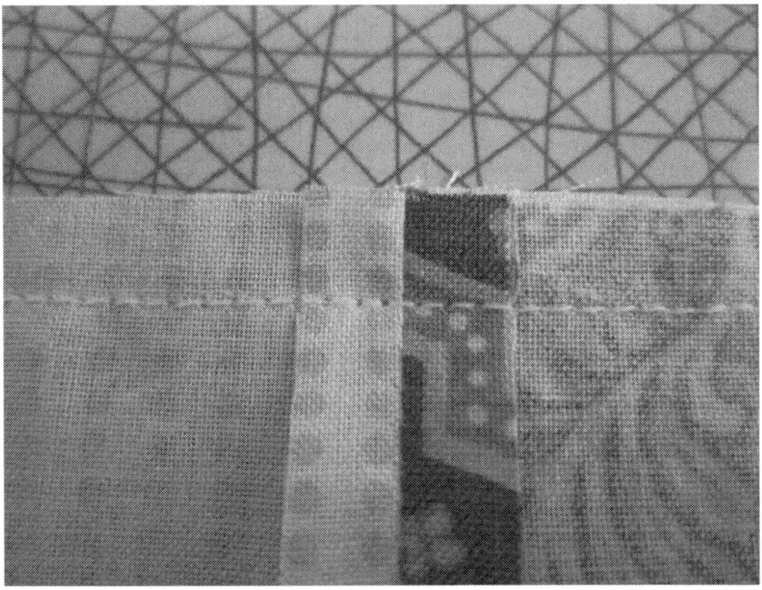

You'll sew the squares into three lines, and afterward sew the lines together. Arrangement is key here!

I will normally spread out the squares in the example I need on my work surface and afterward sew them. That way you have less possibility of sewing an inappropriate bit together in light of the fact that you can perceive how the completed square looks.

Recollect that you are utilizing a 1/4 INCH SEAM ALLOWANCE. (Take a gander at Stage 12 for approaches to make this simple.) : Also, I don't stick the squares together as I sew - don't hesitate to do it from the outset, however trust me, it'll just back you off!

Beginning in the top line, take the initial two squares and sew them right sides together. At that point, sew the last squares right sides along with the center square. You've finished a line! Do the other two thusly. When all the lines are done, finger press the seams open.

At that point, sew the columns together in a similar way, ensuring that the seams line up and lay level. The way to lovely squares is getting all the seams sewn level. The back should seem as though the last picture on the off chance that you've done this accurately.

The photos will assist you with making sense of this in case you're having any issues.

When the squares are sewn, simply stack them and continue sewing until you have 48!

(A note about pressing: I don't do it now. I simply don't. It occupies an excessive amount of time. See the following Stage to find out about finger-squeezing.)

Stage 11: Finger Pressing.

An extremely straightforward method that will accelerate your quilting procedure and give you prettier squares.

When you've sewn a seam, basically flip the material to the posterior, open the seam up, and rake the length of it with your thumbnail.

This will level your seams enough for flawless sewing without getting the iron each moment or something like that.

Stage 12: Guidelines for Getting an Even Seam Allowance.

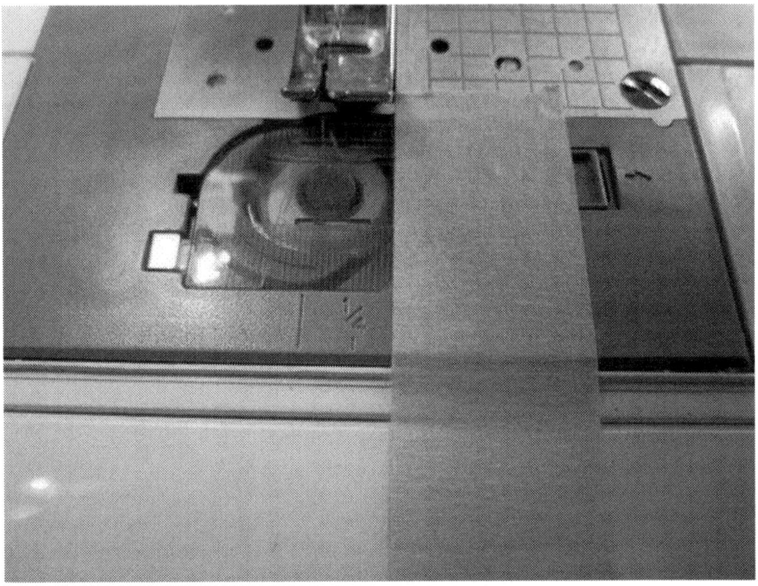

There are numerous apparatuses out there to assist you with ensuring you're sewing at 1/4 inch. :)

There are sewing feet for each sewing machine - the correct edge of the foot is 1/4 inch. You can likewise purchase an attractive sewing guide - however be cautioned, these will possibly work in the event that you have a huge metal surface around your presser foot. A few machines have little throat plates.

The least expensive and most straightforward option is utilizing a bit of concealing tape. Simply stick it on the sewing machine where the edge of the material should deceive get the correct seam remittance, and BAM! While I'm sufficiently fortunate to have a 1/4 inch foot, I likewise use veiling tape for extra certainty.

(I've additionally observed individuals use post-it notes in the event that you don't have any covering tape lying around.)

(Additionally, you'll notice in the picture that 1/4 inch is named on my machine and not being utilized - that is on the grounds that it's off-base. Measure from your needle out in case you're uncertain about the right situation of the tape or different apparatuses.)

Stage 13: Choosing the Final Block Layout.

Iron every one of your squares to get them additional level.

Locate an unfilled bit of floor and spread the squares out. I don't place an excess of thought into this for patchwork quilts. Similarly as long as there aren't such a large number of comparable colors contacting you're all set!

Ensure that the last format is 6 squares wide and 8 squares in length. :)

Stage 14: Pinning and Numbering Columns.

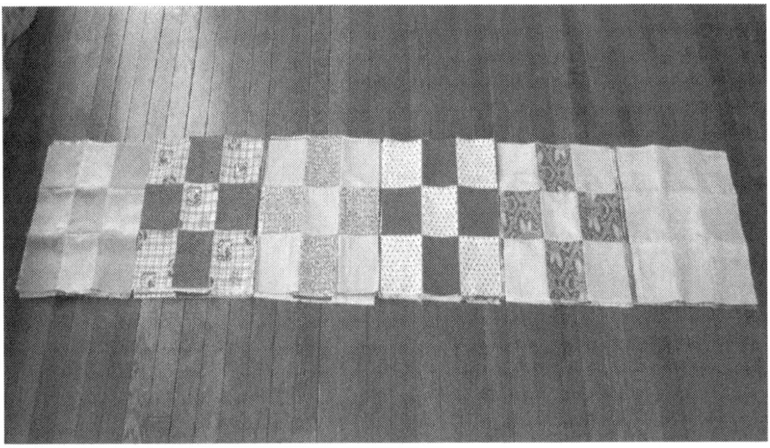

When you have the format chosen, stack the segments in appropriate request and pin the squares together and number the segments. This will assist you with maintaining them in control.

I generally stack them from base to top.

Presently you'll sew the sections together. :)

Stage 15: Sewing together the top of the Quilt, Part one.

You have every one of your squares and you're all set! We are over mostly done at this point! :D

Sew them together square by square to shape sections - I commonly leave my markers on the top squares through this whole procedure so I don't get confounded.

Furthermore, an accommodating clue - when you're up to the 3-4 square in a section, it can get precarious to sew. To cure all the pulling and material going all over the place, move up what you've just sewn as appeared in the last picture. :)

Stage 16: Ironing.

Now, it's useful to press once more. You extremely simply need to concentrate on where the squares meet - make a point to get the seams quite level.

So segregate your cat from the pressing board and get moving. :)

Stage 17: Sewing the Quilt Top Together, Part Two.

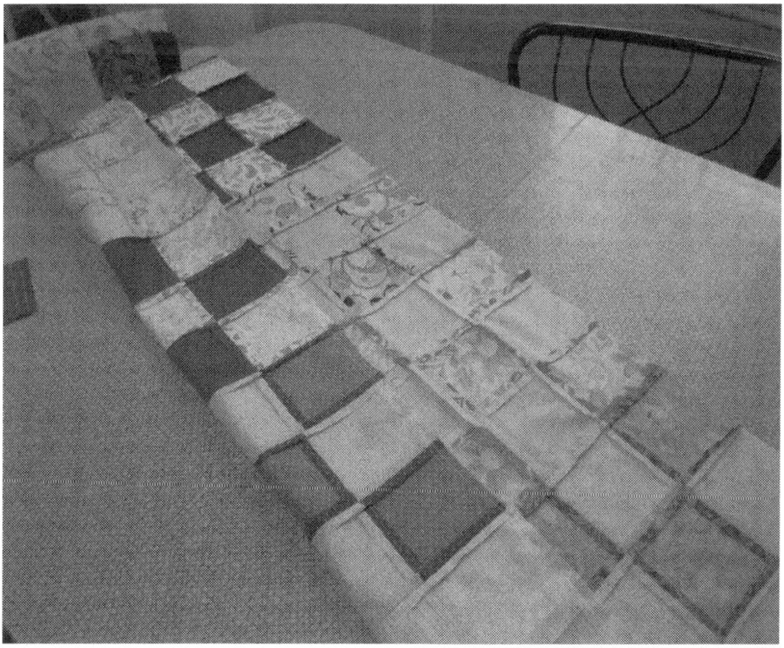

Presently you'll sew the segments together to make the quilt top!

This is the main time I'll stick while sewing the quilt top. Since you're managing much more material and it can move like insane, I pin each couple of squares, as appeared in the subsequent picture. :)

Start by laying section 1 on your stir surface straight up. Lay segment 2 on it, right side down. Line everything up as well as possible, and afterward pin.

To appropriately sew this, get the top corner made sure about in your machine, and heap the remainder of the section into your lap. You don't need any of the material hanging off the table - it causes genuine pulling and will cause you to sew abnormally and places additional weight in your machine. So ensure you're not letting the sewn material heap up behind the machine and the material that is taking care of through is upheld well. In the event that you feel any pulling, quit sewing and modify the material. (Pictures 3 and 4)

Continue sewing on the extra sections until you're done, and recollect that moving proves to be useful! (Picture 6)

Stage 18: You Quilt Top Is Set!

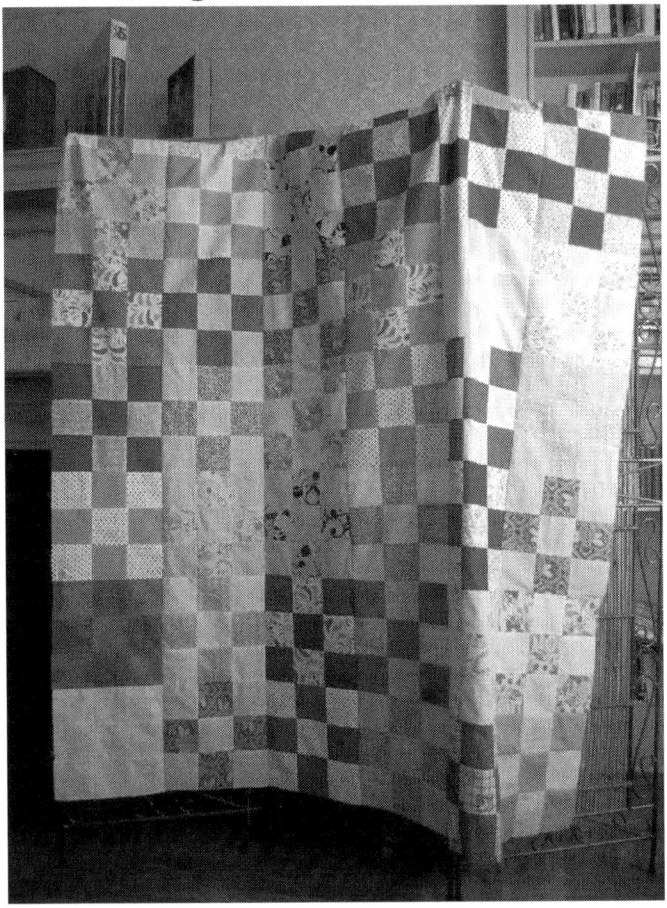

Wonder in your greatness.

Stage 19: Quilt Sandwich - Laying or Setting It Out.

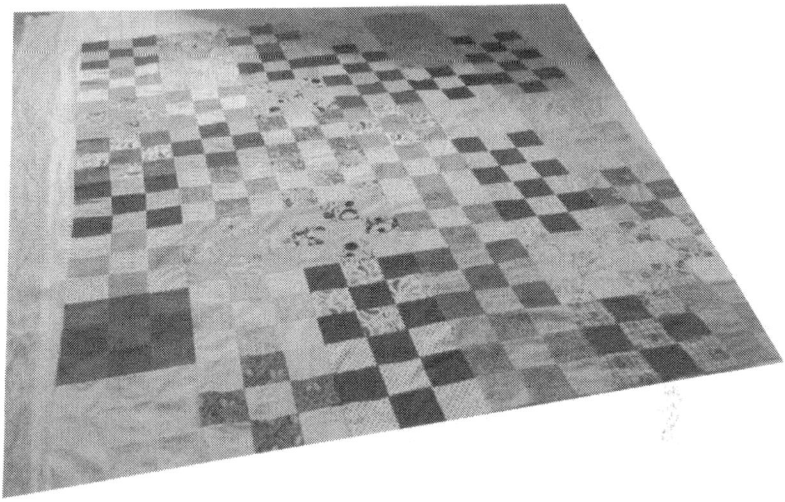

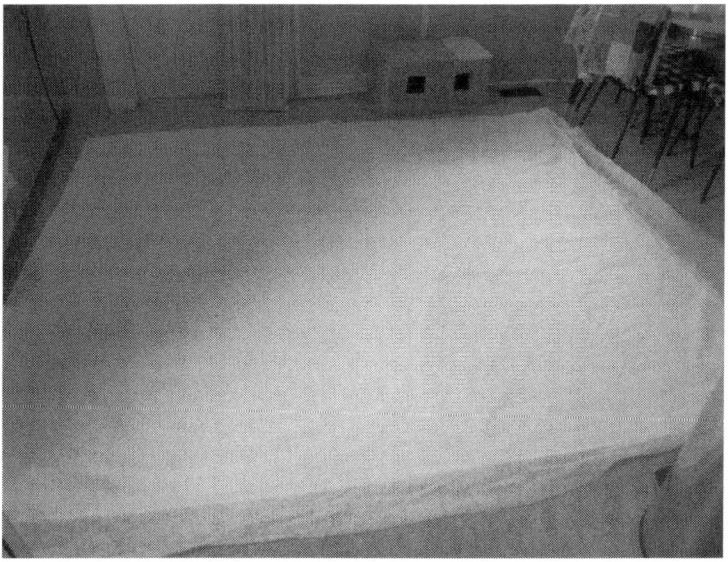

Pick a huge spot on your floor - hardwood or tile is superior to using carpet. At that point clean your floor! This is significant, particularly in case you're utilizing a white backing. Likewise ensure your feet are spotless - you will walk and creeping everywhere throughout the quilt.

(Additionally, shoo all creatures out of the room, in any case picture 2 will occur.)

Iron your backing and spread it out - smooth it out so you have no wrinkles or knocks.

On this, spread out your batting. Smooth it out also, and ensure it's focused on your backing.

Presently, lay your quilt top down. Ensure everything is focused and smooth it out.

The most ideal approach to streamline it is to get down on all fours, sincerely. You can either go start to finish or from the center out. Do what works best for you - simply make certain to be exceptionally intensive!

When it's streamlined it's an ideal opportunity to stick it!

Stage 20: Quilt Sandwich - Pinning and Trimming.

You need to stick through every one of the three layers around the outside of the quilt.

When the outside is stuck, trim all around the edges. I regularly leave two or three creeps on each side.

(Also, keep the surplus material from the sheet - we will utilize that to produce the binding!)

Presently, in case you're truly stressed that you may have knocks - flip the quilt over and look at the back once it's stuck around the edges.

For this situation, my sheet wasn't having any desire to get along (see the knocks on picture 3?), so I stuck and smoothed once again. When you're fulfilled, flip it back finished and pin like a mad person.

Truly, pin everywhere. The more pins you have, the smoother it'll remain while sewing. For whatever length of time that your pins are in squares, you'll be fine. :)

Stage 21: Getting ready for Quilting.

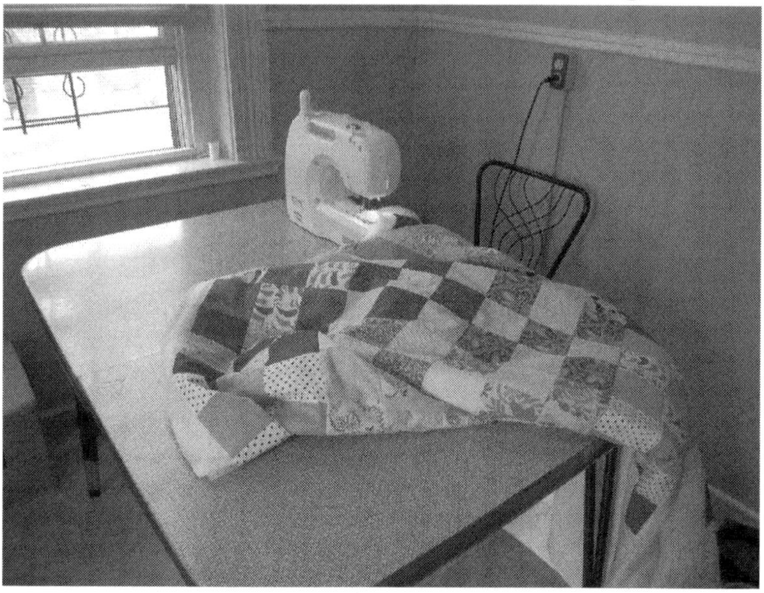

You should trade out the string for sewing. The spool (the string at the highest point of your machine) will be clear nylon, and the string stacked into the bobbin will be white cotton. (Or on the other hand whatever shading will coordinate your support or backing.) Set your line length to the longest.

(Note that you can keep it white cotton on both - yet I'm not a fan. Having clear nylon on top will camouflage your fastens so you don't need to stress over conflicting with the material colors.)

When you have the string stacked, it's in every case great to do a trial of fastens on a bit of scrap material - you may need to change your machine settings a piece.

Likewise, it's additionally a smart thought to change out your needle - you'll require another sharp one since you'll be experiencing different layers!

The best set-okay with sewing is putting your sewing machine at the very edge of a table so the quilt has some place to go as you sew it. The quilt that hasn't experienced the machine yet will lie on your lap. Attempt your hardest to not let the quilt dangle from the table - this can cause lopsided fastens and make your sewing machine work a lot harder.

Stage 22: The Walking Foot.

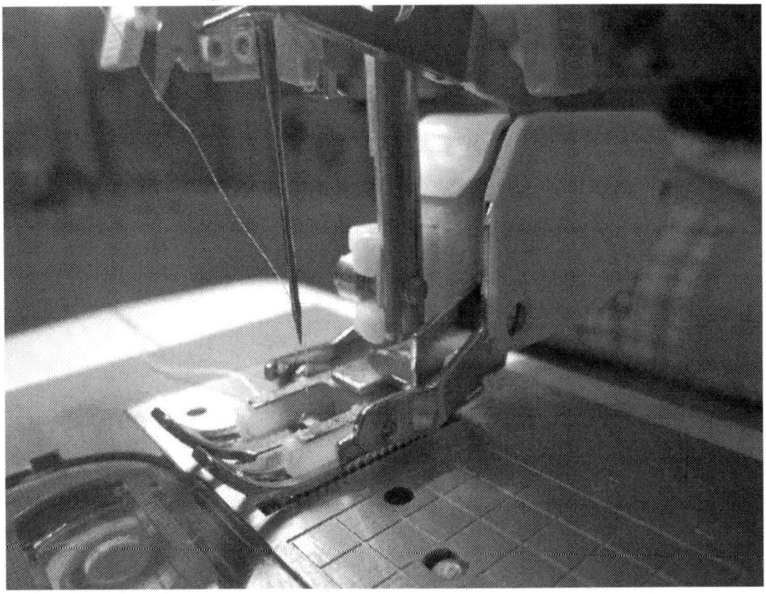

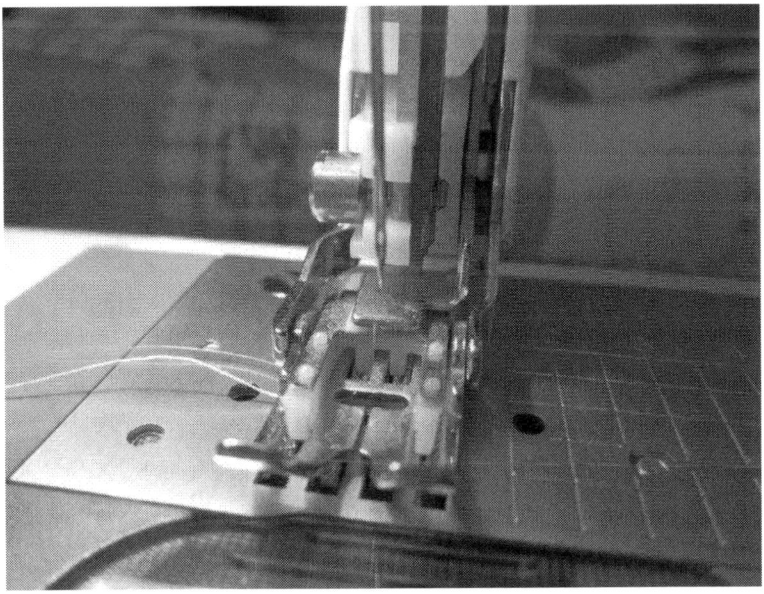

This is the finest of all quilting accessories.

I exceptionally, strongly suggest utilizing a mobile foot for quilting. A mobile foot looks somewhat like something out of Star Wars, however it does ponders for keeping your materials in line. It works like the feed hounds under the needle that get the material through - just on top! So you get extra leveling pulling power which keeps the join from getting stressed and small, and shields your material from puckering and ruching a crazy sum!

I endeavored to sew half of the quilt utilizing my standard presser foot (to make sure I could state, "Hello, it's alright, utilize a customary foot!") and the backing material will experience an exciting day, moved something dreadful.

So I'll be cutting the quilt a piece, not a serious deal. :)

In any case, simply be cautioned... a mobile foot will make your life simpler. :

Stage 23: Quilting!

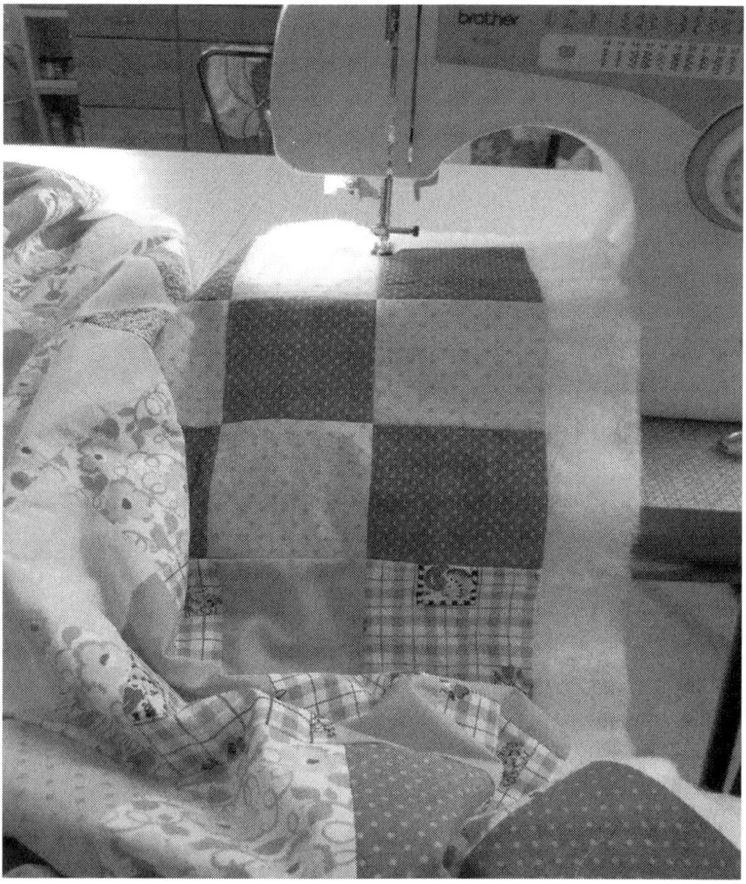

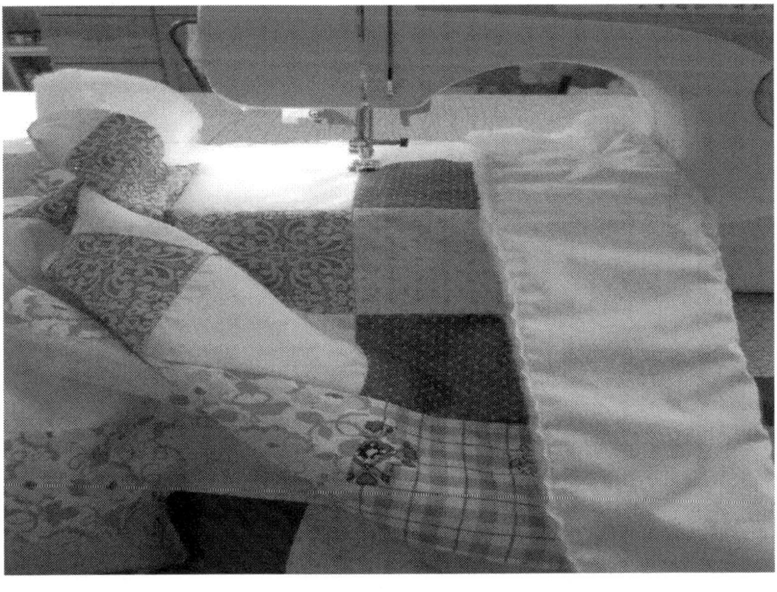

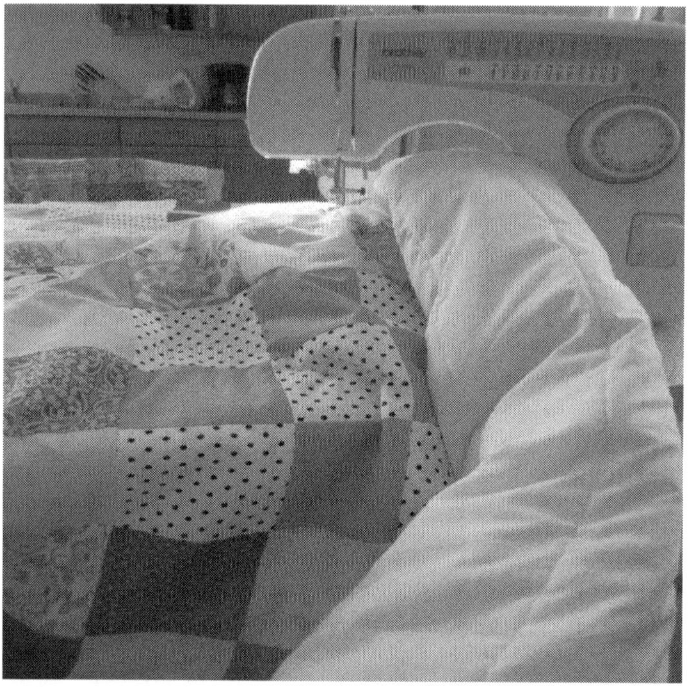

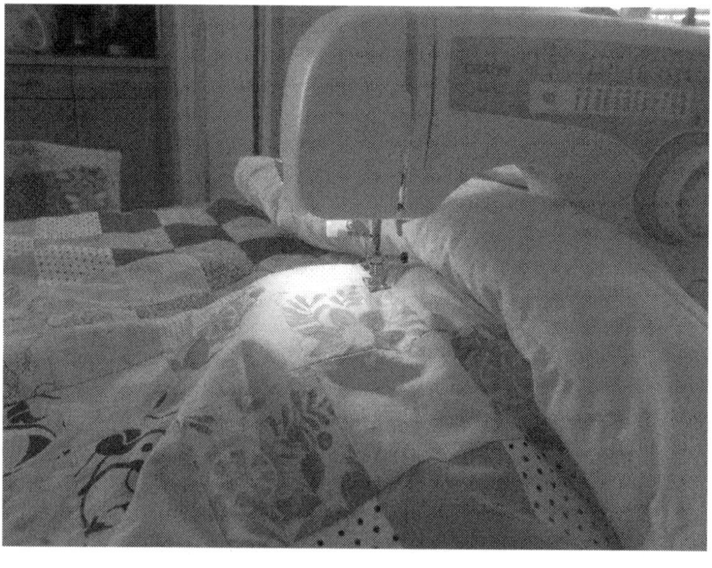

We will do this the simplest conceivable way since I'm accepting a great many people doing this will have an itty bitty sewing machine like me which makes it truly difficult to accomplish progressively complex stuff. :)

All we will do is sewing over the seam lines, which will make a pleasant puffy network. (Otherwise called sewing in the discard!)

You'll begin sewing the quilt straight up, on the correct side. The first side that you should sew first is the long side. You don't need to backstitch for this, either, so don't stress over that.

I generally sew straight down the primary seam in the first place, and afterward you can sew the very edge of the quilt together on the off chance that you like. At that point you can return to sewing in the jettison. Keep on doing this for the following couple lines. Evacuate your pins after you sew the seam to one side of them.

At this point you'll see you have a lot of material packing up on the privilege against your sewing machine - the least demanding approach to battle this is to roll the quilt up on the privilege so you can continue sewing. You'll continue moving it until you get midway and afterward flip the quilt so you're sewing the opposite side. Keep sewing and moving until you finish all the seams.

At that point, turn the quilt with the goal that you're sewing down the short side and replicate - sew and move until the center, and afterward flip and sew and roll once more.

How simple was that? :)

Stage 24: How Your Quilt Should Appear After Quilting

Your completed quilt will basically resemble a puffy grid. This is simpler to see on the back. Odds are you have a ton of little puckers in the material and this is alright. It's my conclusion that a patchwork unique quilt should LOOK like it was made at home. Every one of those little puckers give it character!

Now, if you're backing material has moved, or all the layers didn't arrange somehow or another, simply trim a little off the edges of the quilt. This occurs, and by and by, it's alright! (What's more, in addition, in the event that you have a little machine like me, or you don't utilize a mobile foot, some moving is nearly ensured to happen!)

Additionally remember that once you wash the quilt the first run through the puckers will level out and it will look emphatically beautiful since you didn't prewash the materials. :)

Stage 25: Creating the Binding, Part One.

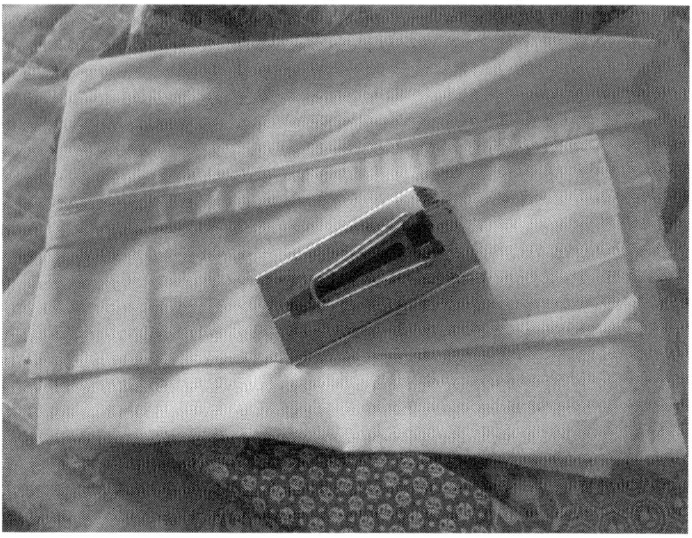

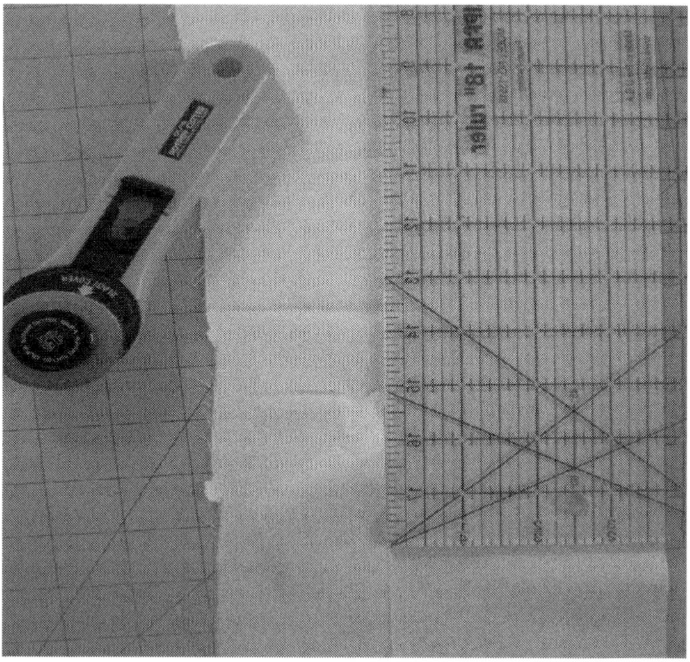

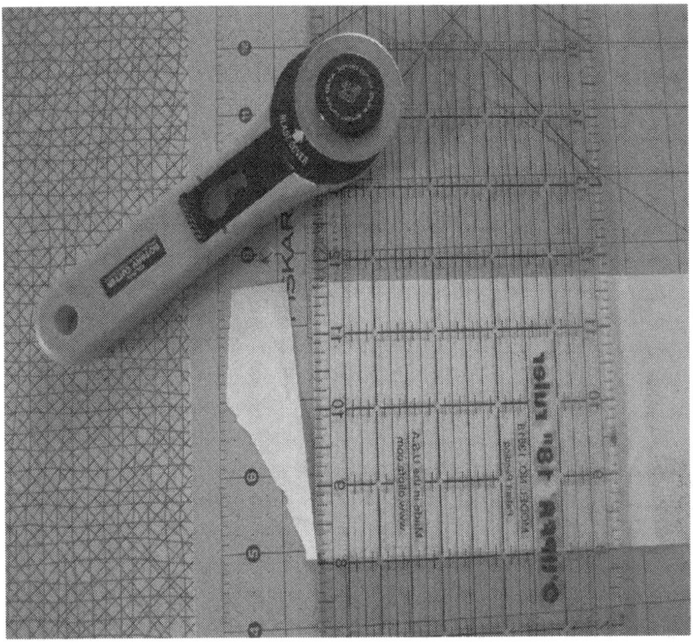

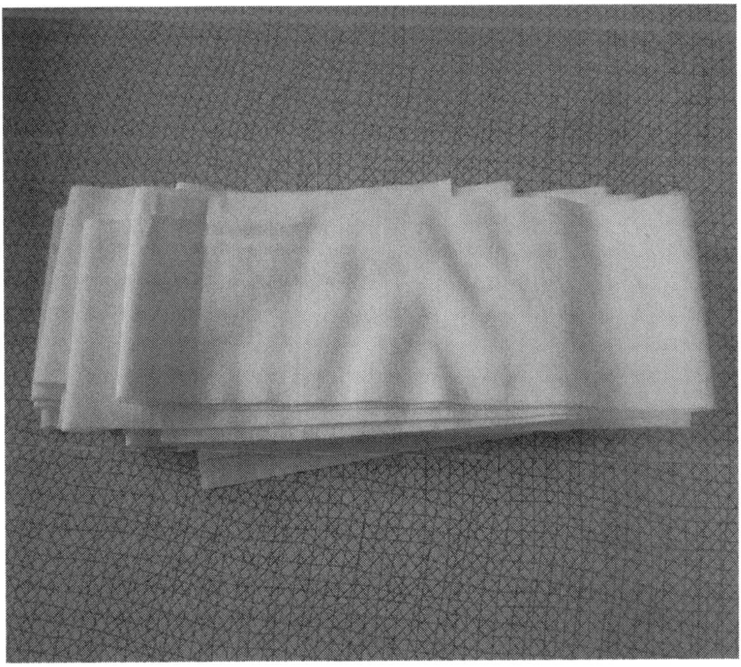

There are a two different ways to do this - you can purchase bias tape from the store or you can utilize the excess from the sheet. I'm demonstrating how to utilize the excess from the sheet since bias tape is costly and I'm on a tight spending plan. :)

The main thing you have to do is to cut your sheet into strips. I am utilizing a 2 inch bias tape creator, so I will be cutting my sheet into 3/4 inch strips, trying to make right the parts of the bargains.

(Note that I generally cut straight strips. I may be utilizing a bias tape creator, however I don't cut the material on the bias - I cut on the straight grain. I haven't had any issues with my binding tiring along these lines. I simply needed to clear that up in light of the fact that I had an inquiry in the remarks about it.)

Stage 26: Creating the Binding, Part two.

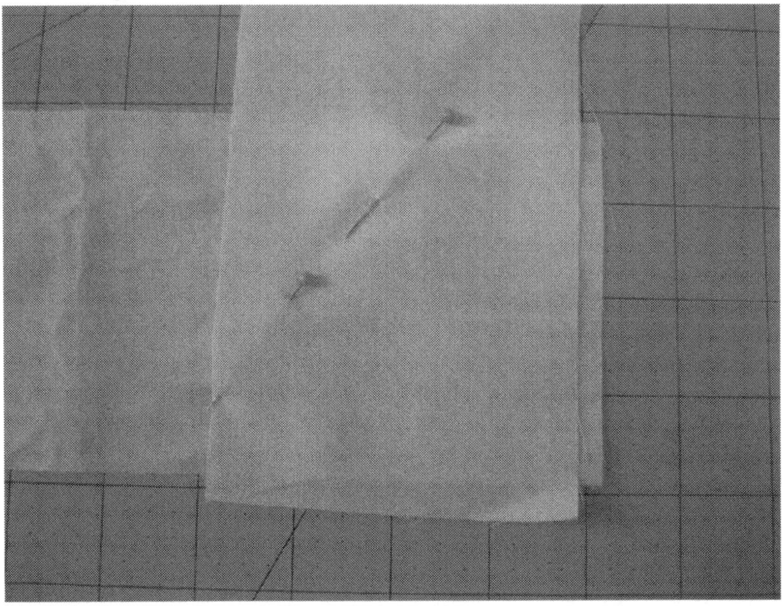

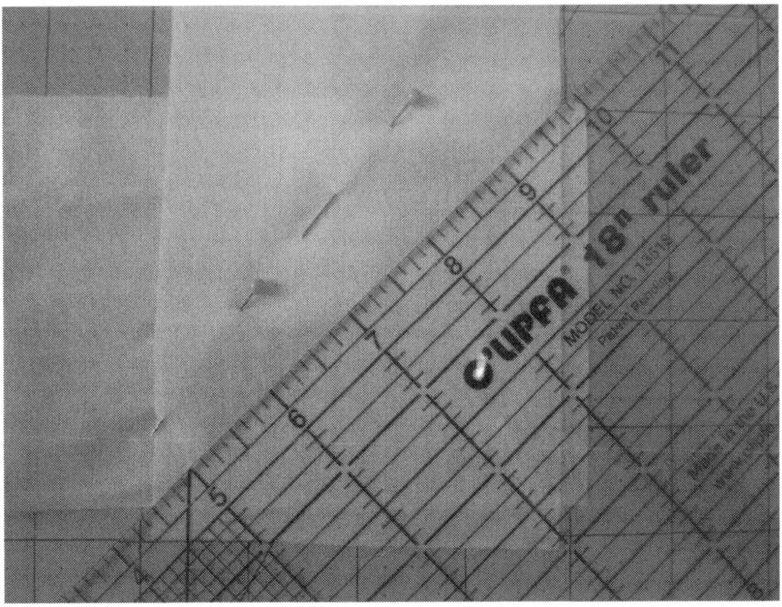

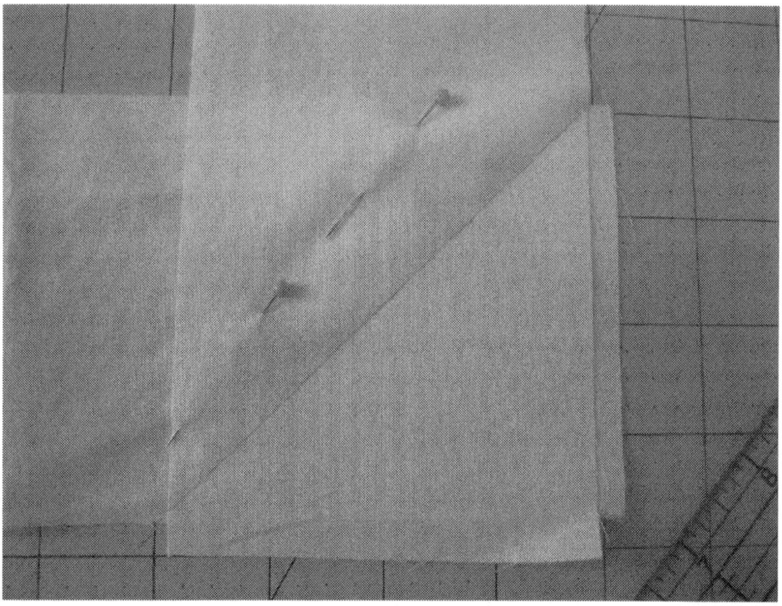

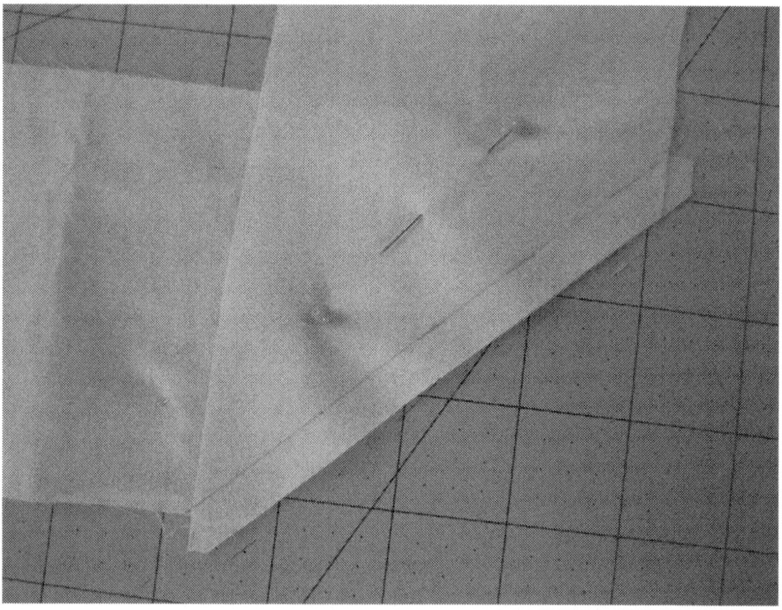

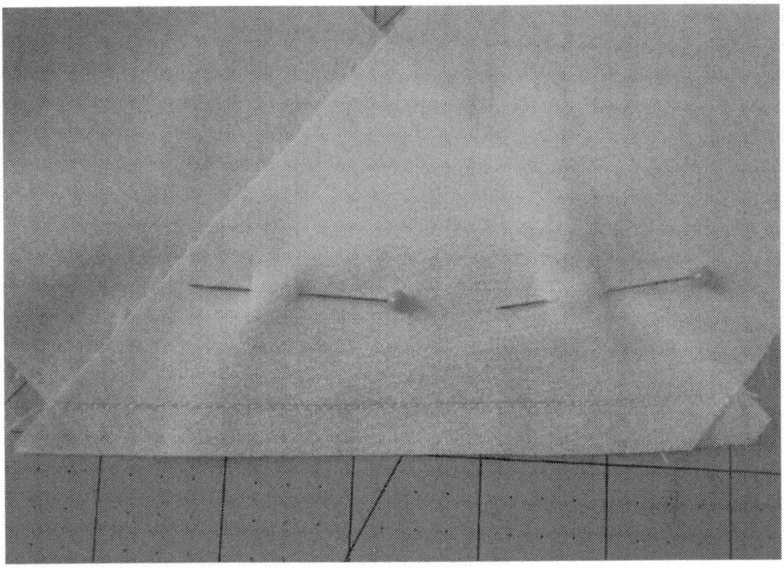

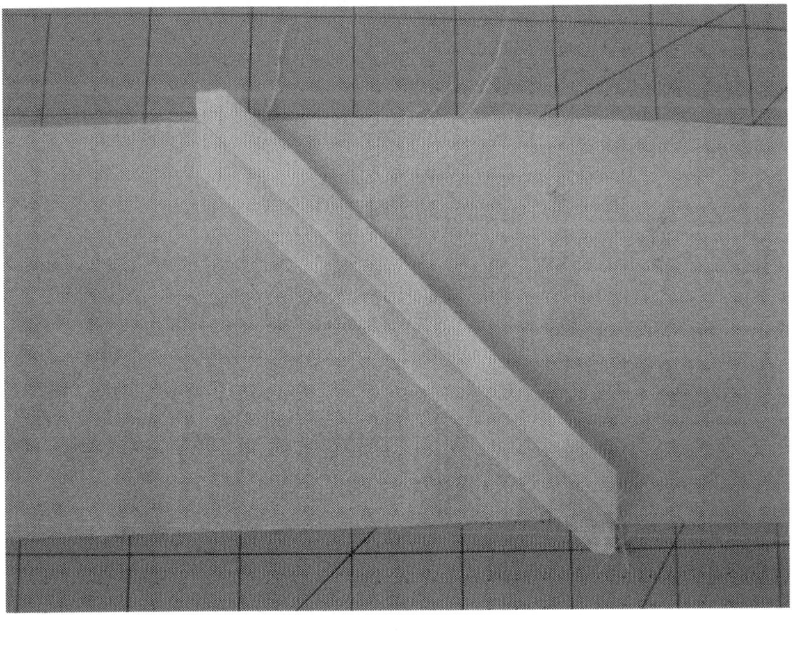

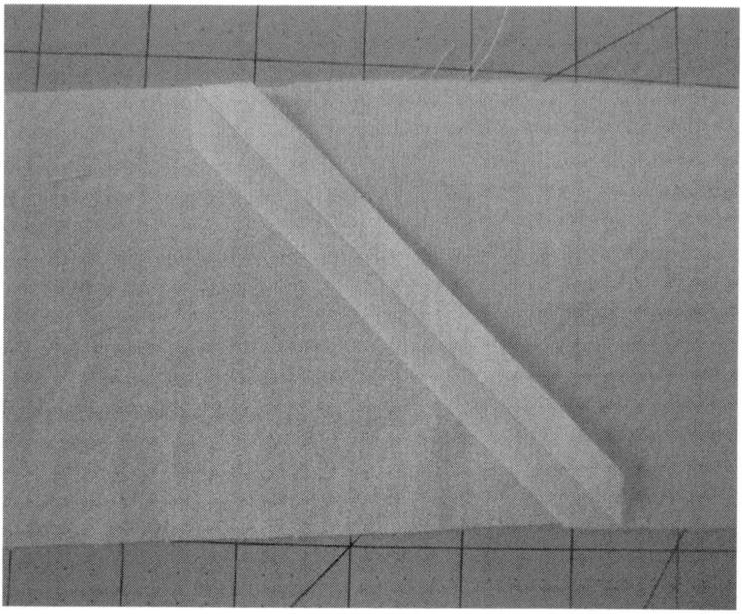

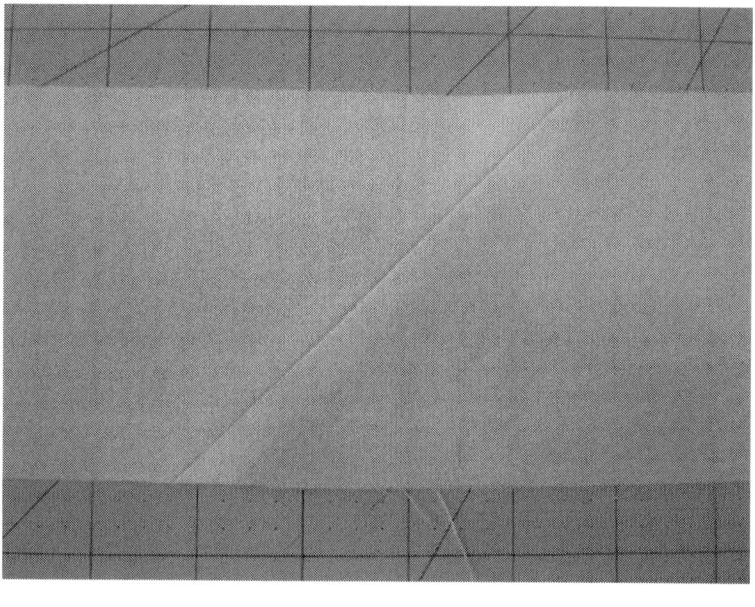

You'll have to switch back to the standard presser foot for this.

Presently we sew the strips together! Take two strips and lay them on your work surface as appeared in the primary picture and pin. Presently take your ruler and draw a slanting line. Remove the surplus material.

Sew along the line you drew and afterward press the seam level.

When it's squeezed, remove the bits hanging out!

Keep sewing your strips together until you have enough to go right around your quilt + and extra foot or somewhere in the vicinity.

Stage 27: Creating the Bias Tape, Part Three.

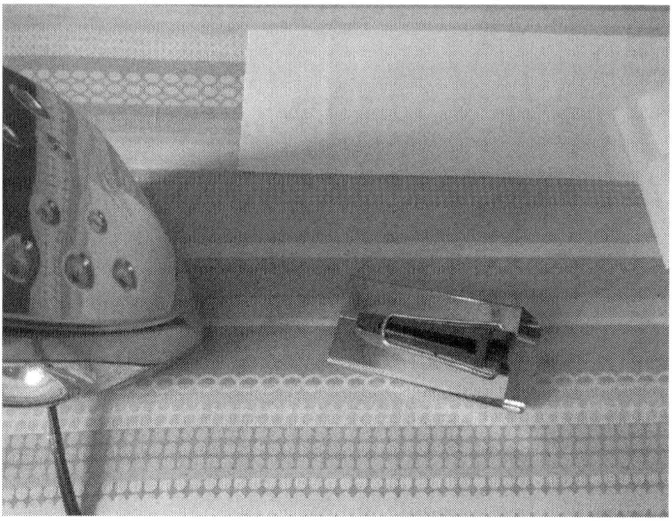

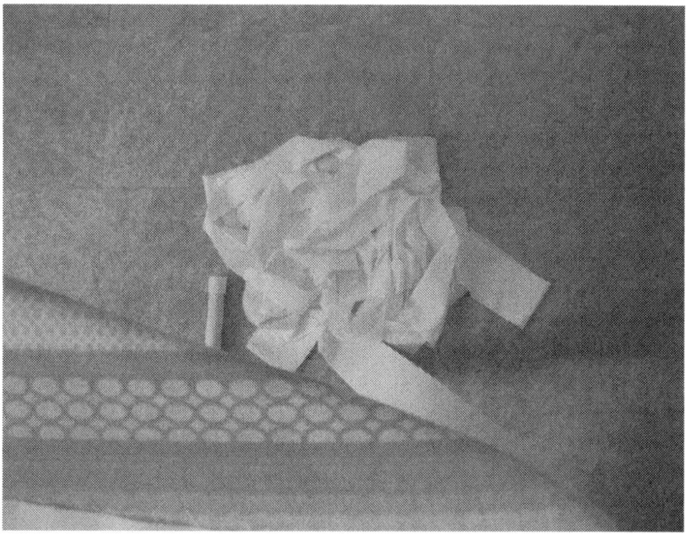

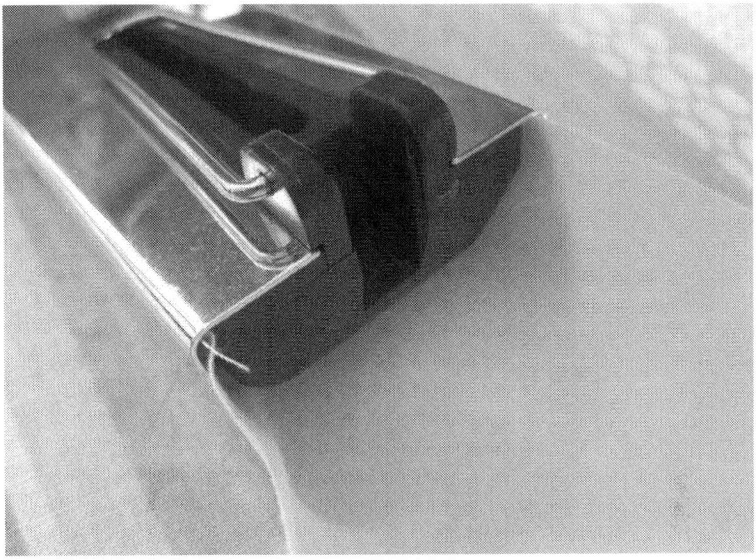

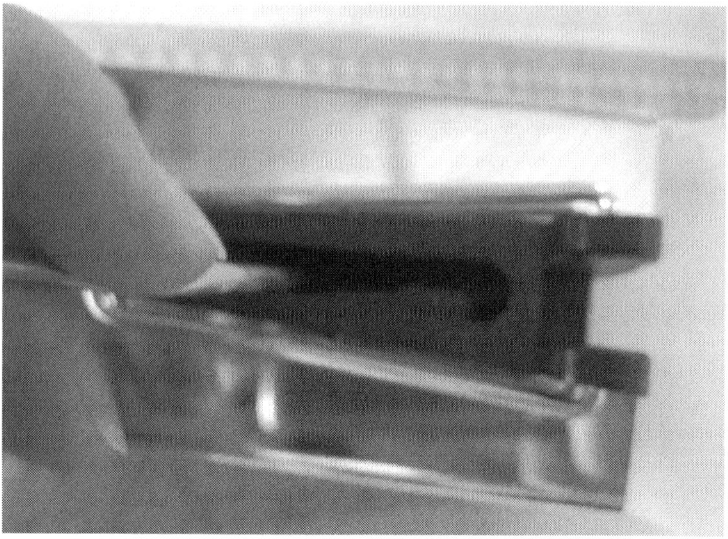

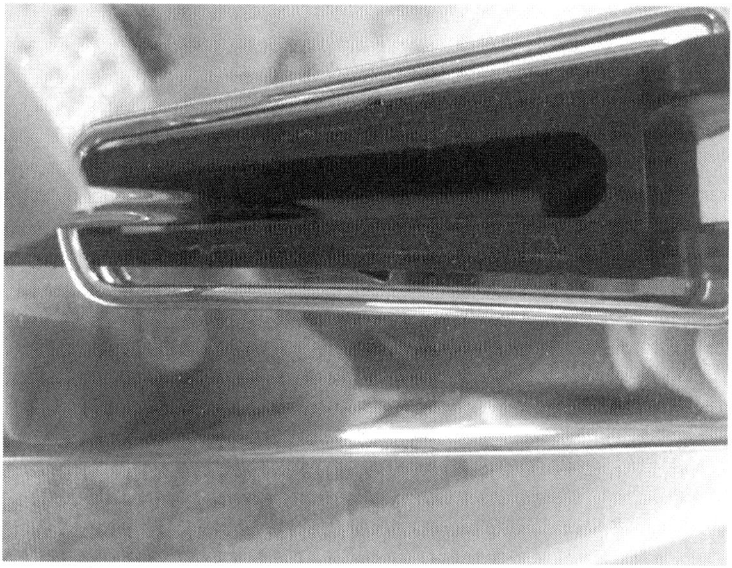

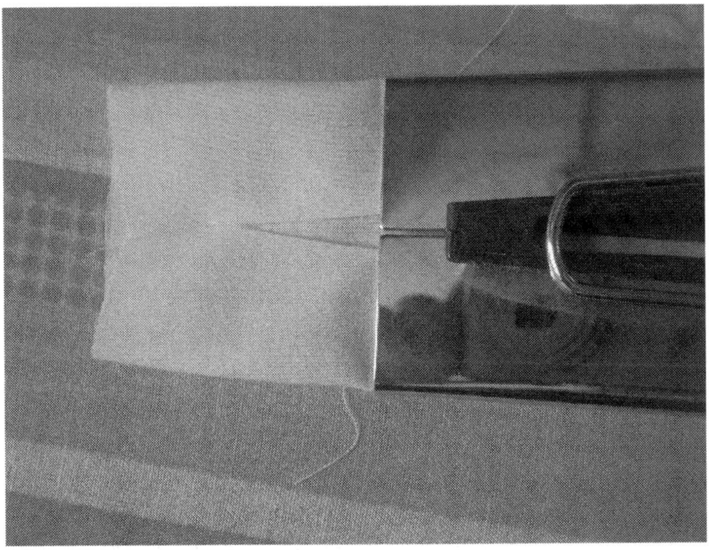

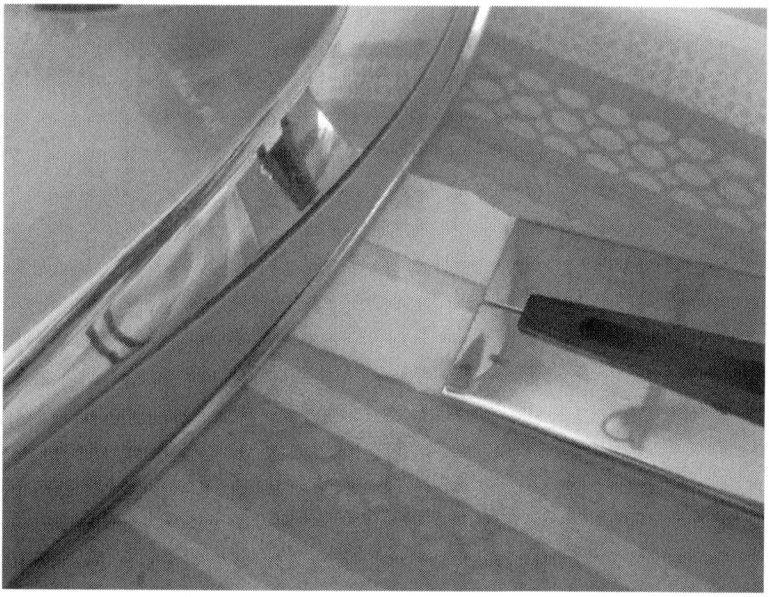

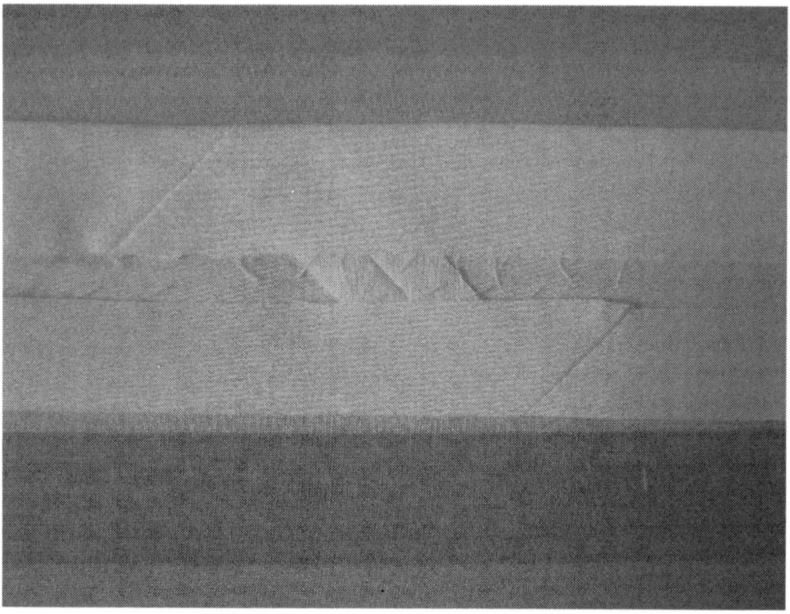

The last part!!! Yippee!

Get out your pressing board, iron, bias tape producer, and bring your tremendous piece of material... what's more, you can suspend that off the finish of the pressing board as found in picture two.

Feed the material into the bias tape maker wrong side up (with the goal that you can see the base of the seams) and push it in until you can see the material through the opening in the center. Discover something small (I utilized a little stitch snare) to stick into the opening and drag the tape through. When it's out you're all set!

Hold the completed bias tape down and drag the bias tape creator the other way and iron the new bias tape that structures. Feed the bias tape off the far edge of the pressing board from the material strip.

Ensure the seams feed through quite level and that your material doesn't bundle up in the bias tape producer and you ought to be fine!

When you've taken care of everything through and pressed it overall quite level, seam the bias tape down the middle and iron it once more!

Presently you're done!

Stage 28: Ensuring Your Quilt is superb and well Trimmed!

On the off chance that you had any moving or bizarreness, right now is an ideal opportunity to make things overall quite square. Above are photos of my quilt after I cut it. :)

Simply ensure every one of your layers is even.

Stage 29: Affixing the Binding to Your Quilt.

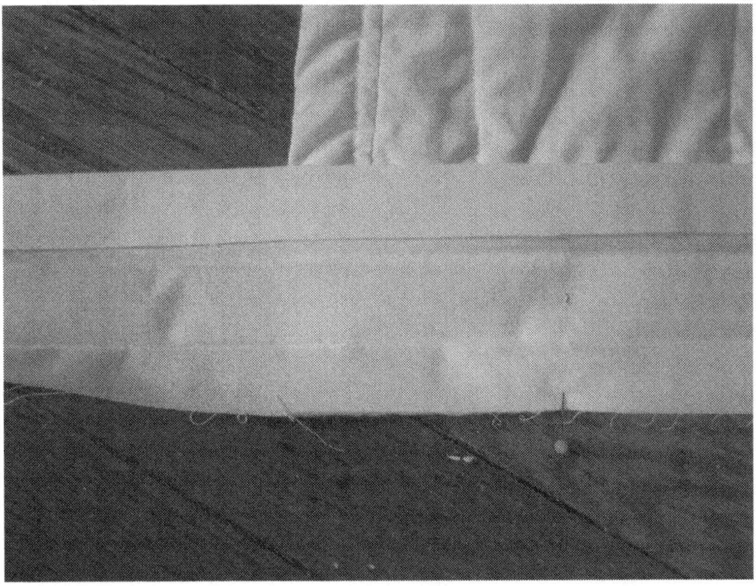

Incorporates the magnificent fold for getting excellent, simple corners.

What you have to do is open up one edge of the bias tape with the goal that you can see the crude edges. You'll arrange this crude edge according to the edge of your quilt.

Beginning on one of the long sides of the quilt around the center, pin the crude edge of the bias tape to the edge of the quilt, leaving a 6 inch tail of bias tape. Keep sticking each six inches or so until you arrive at the corner.

At the corner, broaden the bias tape over the reverse edge. At that point, overlap it back with the goal that it shapes a triangle and goes to one side the first stuck strip. Presently, seam the strip back over the triangle so the collapsed edge lines up with the crude edge and the strip would now be able to proceed down the shorter side of the quilt! (In the event that you've done this effectively, you'll have a little triangle overlap as appeared in the last photograph.

Do this for each corner, and continue sticking each six inches or so until you come around to your beginning Stage. When you arrive at your beginning Stage, pin the bias tape about around 3 inches from where you started and leave a tail of six inches or something like that. Cut the bias tape and you're prepared to sew!

(It would be ideal if you note that my camera failed to capture these photographs, so I'm doing these photos on the completed quilt.)

Stage 30: Sewing the Binding, the Backside.

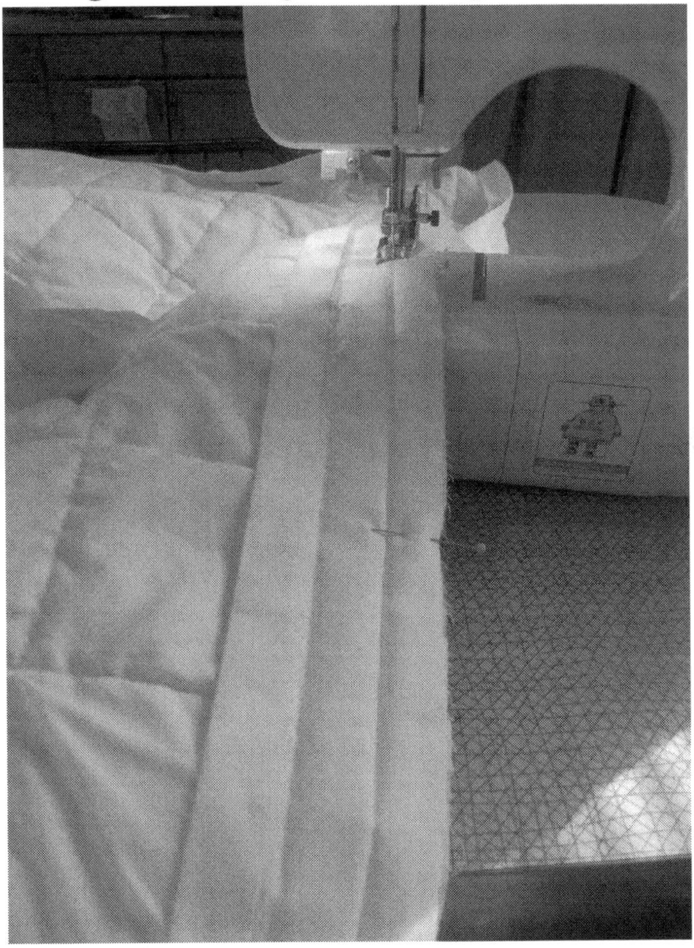

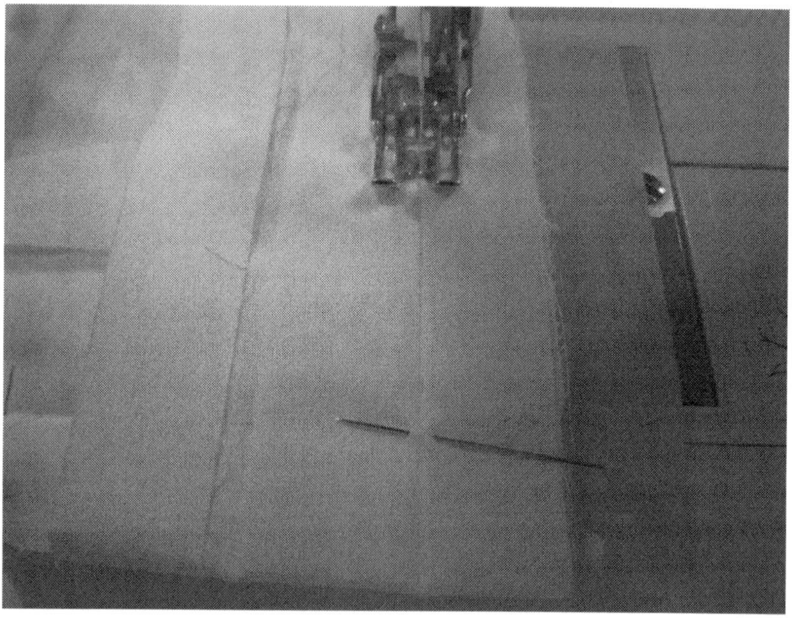

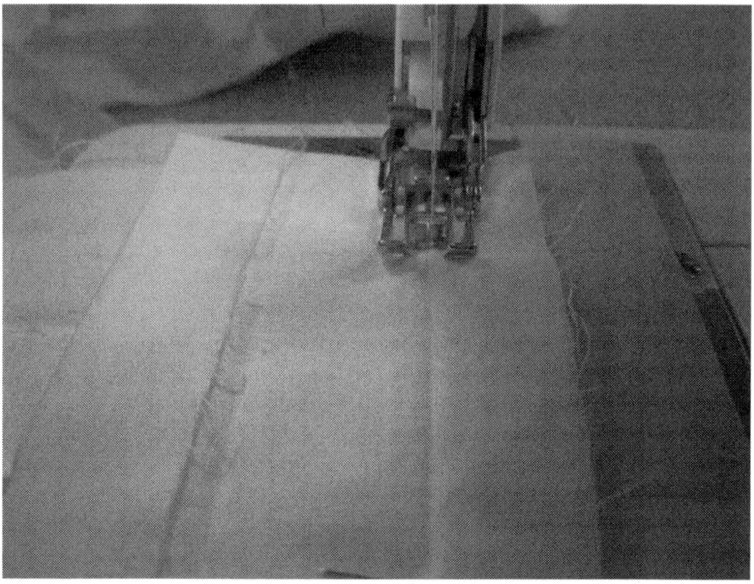

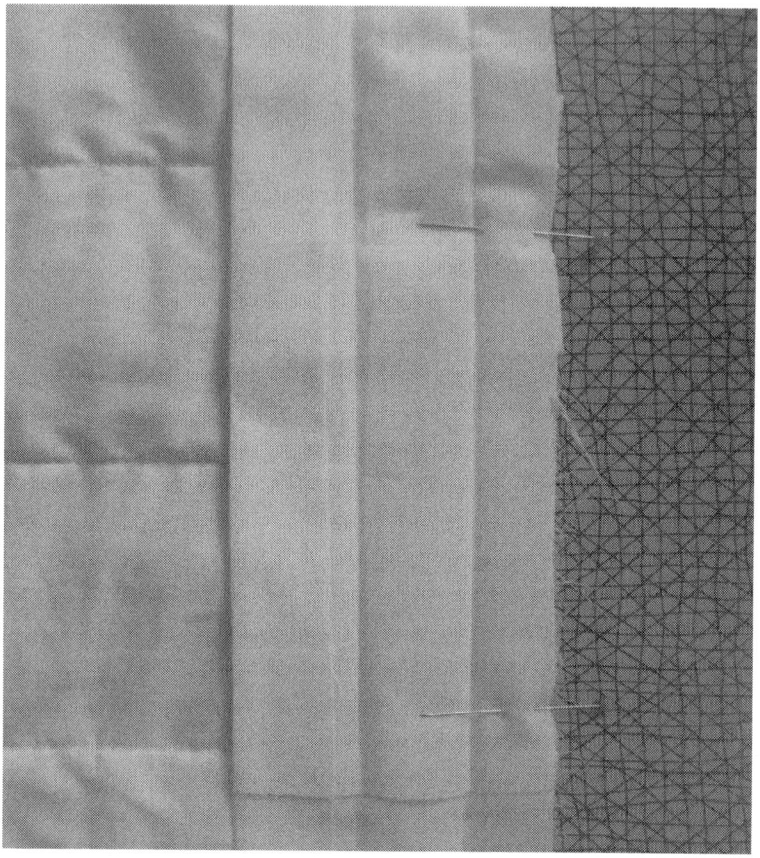

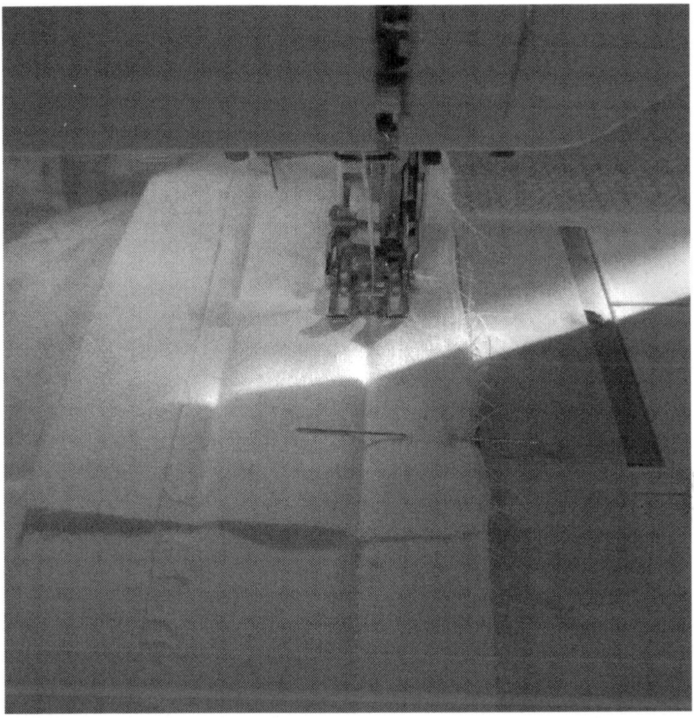

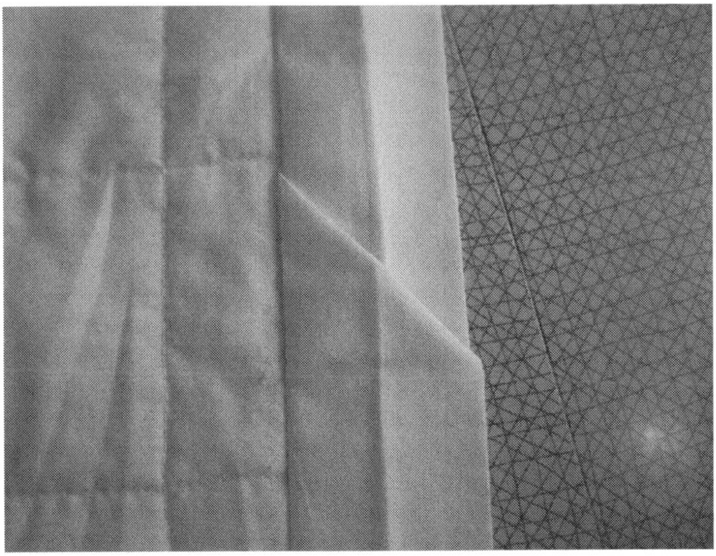

Utilize a standard foot for this! What's more, make a point to take out your pins directly before you get to them. Sewing over pins isn't acceptable. :)

We will join the wrinkle as appeared in the main picture. So join fasten line until you get a couple of inches from the main corner. The corners are just somewhat tricky.

At the point when you get close to the corner, quit sewing and take a pin. Recall the insane overlap we made? Run your finger along the wrinkle line until you can feel the triangle seam underneath (picture 2) and imprint that place with a pin (picture 3). This is the place you will quit sewing. Sew to that point, backstitch, and expel the quilt from the machine. Picture 4 shows what it ought to resemble. Presently, flip over the triangle overlap so it covers the join you simply made. (Picture 5)

Presently your wrinkle line is in the opportune spot to continue sewing! Whoopee!

So continue going from the earliest starting point of this wrinkle, and backstitch toward the beginning. Proceed with these means until you get as far as possible.

Sew to where you set the last pin, and backstitch. Expel the quilt from the machine.

Presently the last part! (Picture 7)

Overlap over the base surplus as appeared in picture 8. Lay the top surplus over it, arranging the crude edges, and pin. Presently remove the base excess. (Picture 9)

Starting where you quit sewing at the top, backstitch and sew to where you started sewing the in earliest reference point, back quilting once more. Picture 10 shows what the completed seam resembles - overall quite spotless!

Presently you're prepared to flip the bias tape over!

Stage 31: Flipping and Affixing the Binding.

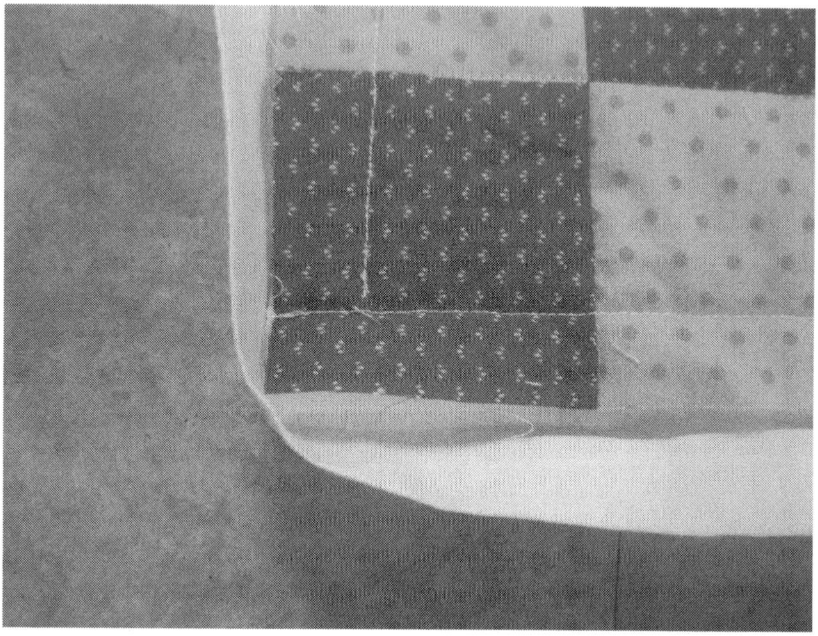

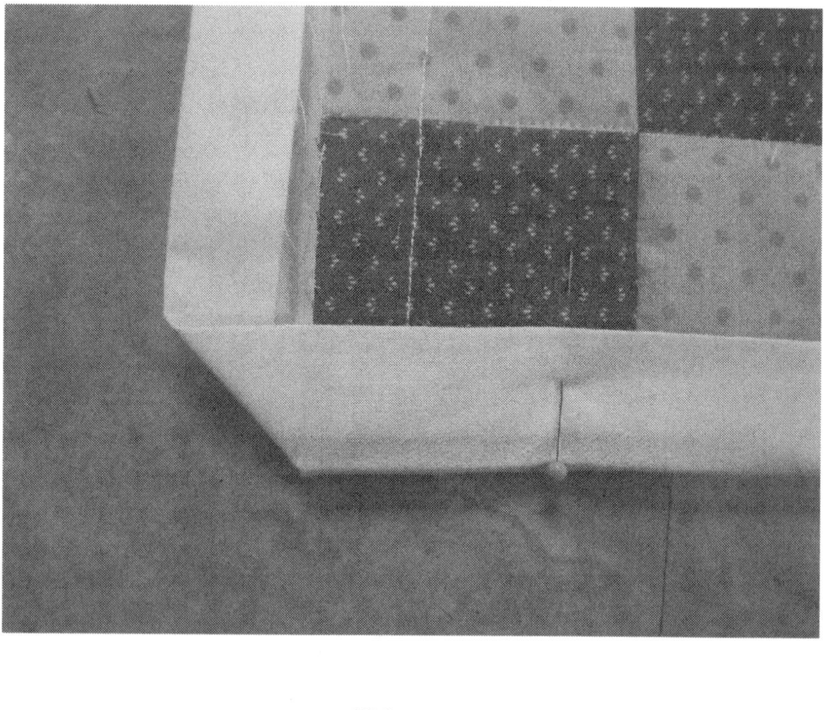

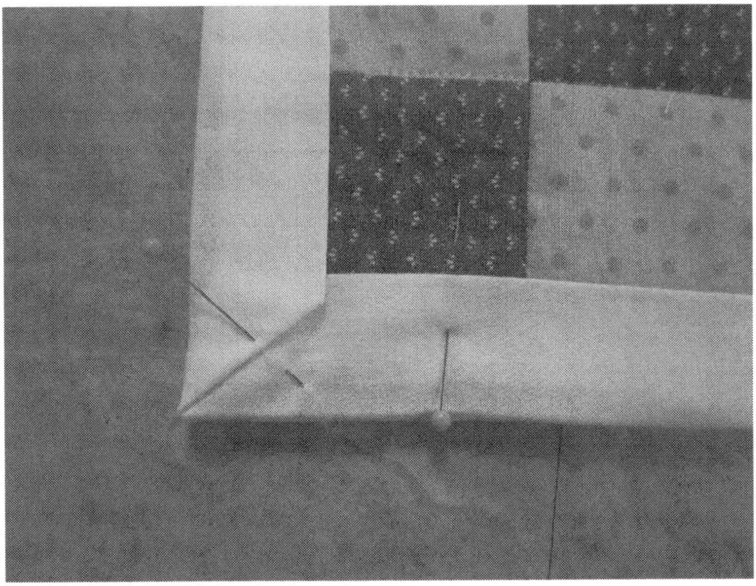

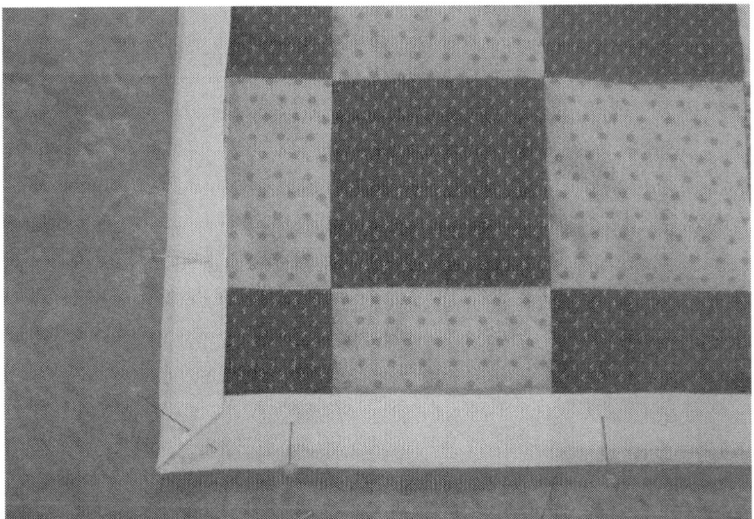

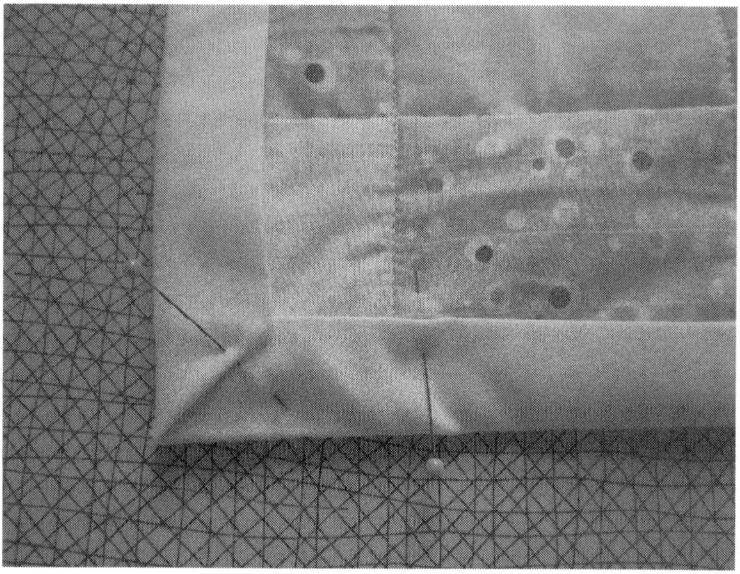

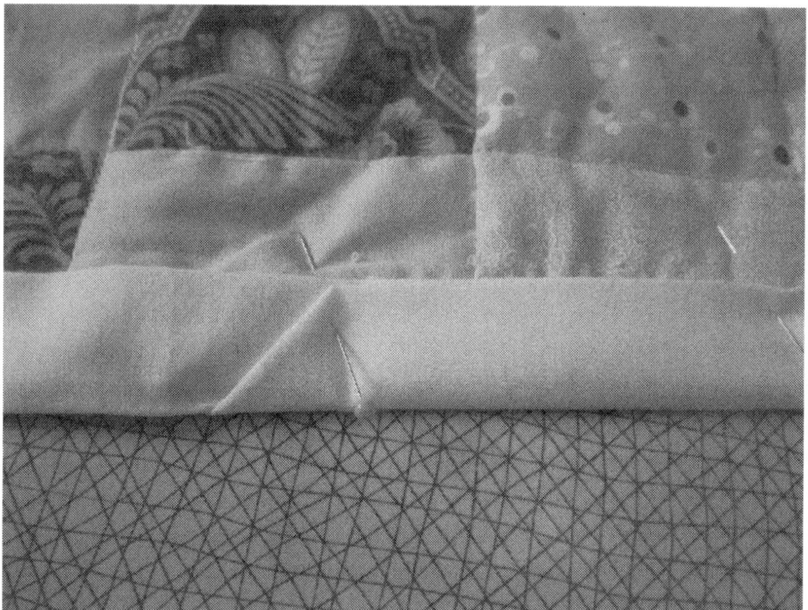

First up - the magnificence of mitered corners... you need to do essentially nothing to the rear of the quilt. Look at the primary picture - how magnificent is that?

The greatest thing to concentrate on when sticking the binding to the front is to conceal the line lines from connecting the bias tape to the back. Try to pull it over that and afterward pin. Those stitch lines can be seen from the second picture)

For the remainder of the corners, just seam up one side, at that point overlay over the other. (As appeared in photographs 2-6)

Photograph 7 tells the best way to reign in where the two parts of the bargains tape meet - simply continue meddling with it until the edges get together and everything looks decent, and afterward pin!

Stage 32: Sewing the Binding, the Front.

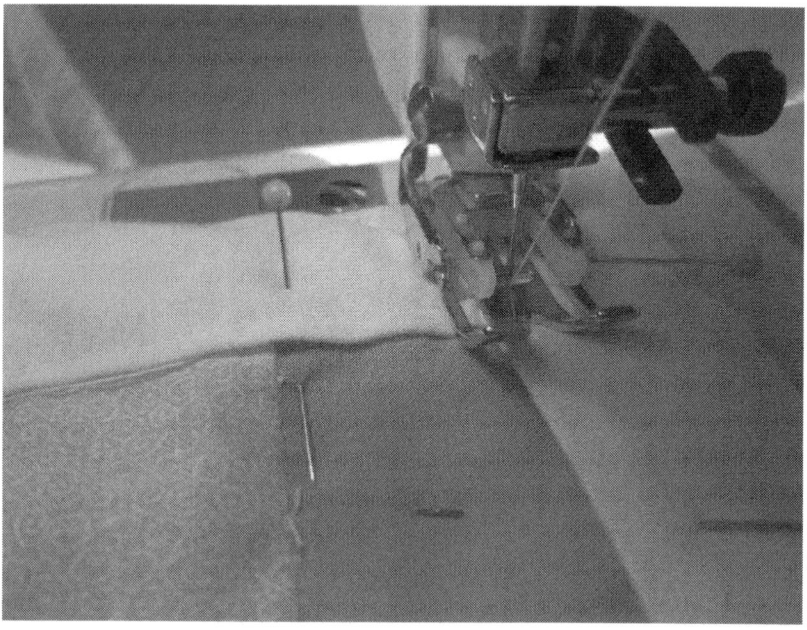

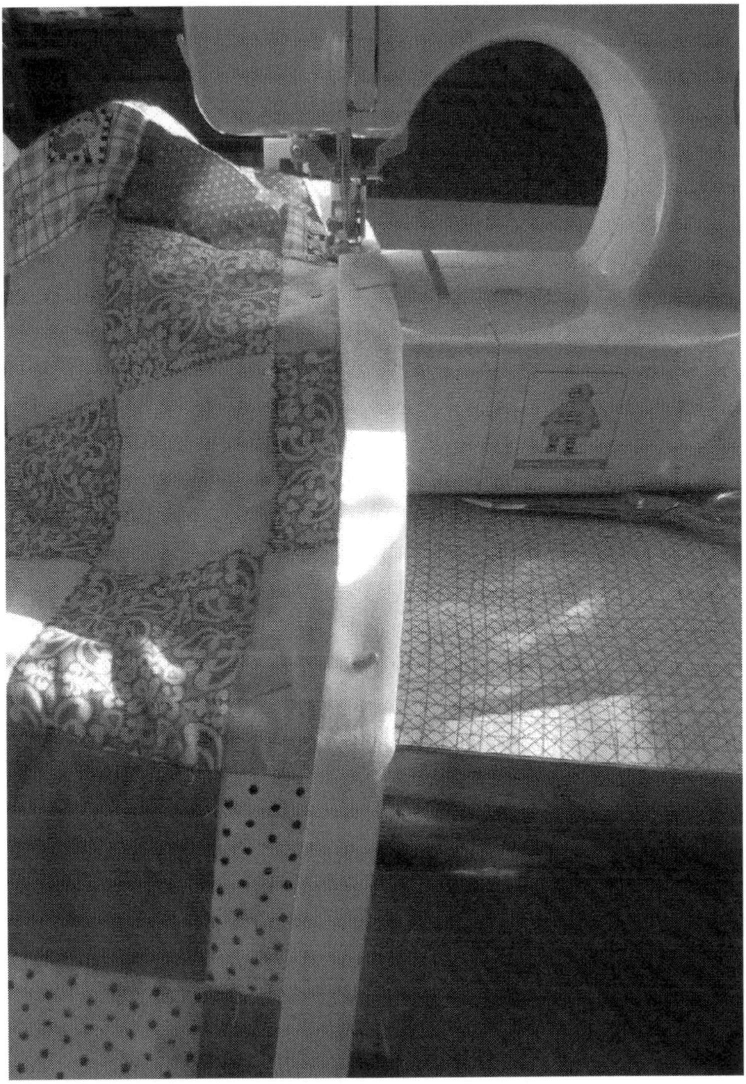

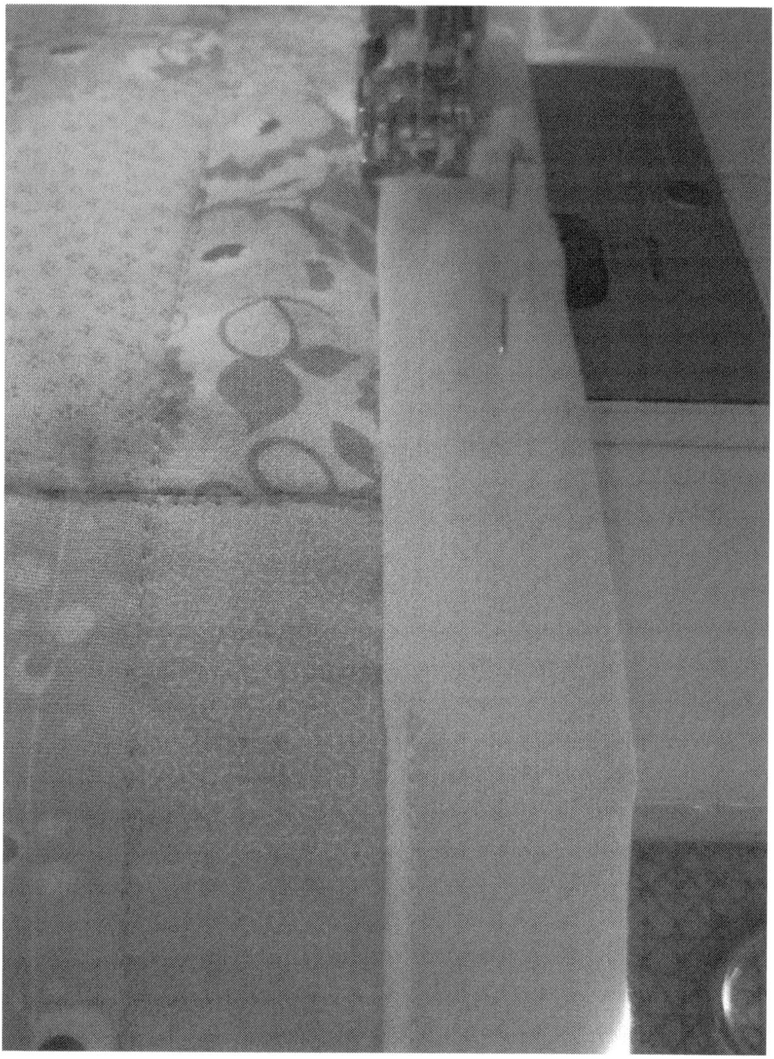

Change out to your walking foot!

You'll be sewing the binding on in one consistent line! Start any place you need, quite near within edge of the binding. You need a 1/4 inch seam allowance or less for this. Make sure to backstitch toward the start and take the pins out as you come to them.

At the point when you get to the corners, leave the needle in the material, raise the presser foot, and swing the material around so you can fight the good fight.

Ensure that you're keeping the bias tape in line... now and then it jumps at the chance to meander. Check it now and again in light of the fact that you need every one of those fastens secured!

As you come around to where you began sewing (picture 4) make a point to arrange your stitch lines and backstitch.

You're finished!!!

Stage 33: More Photographs of the Finished Quilt.

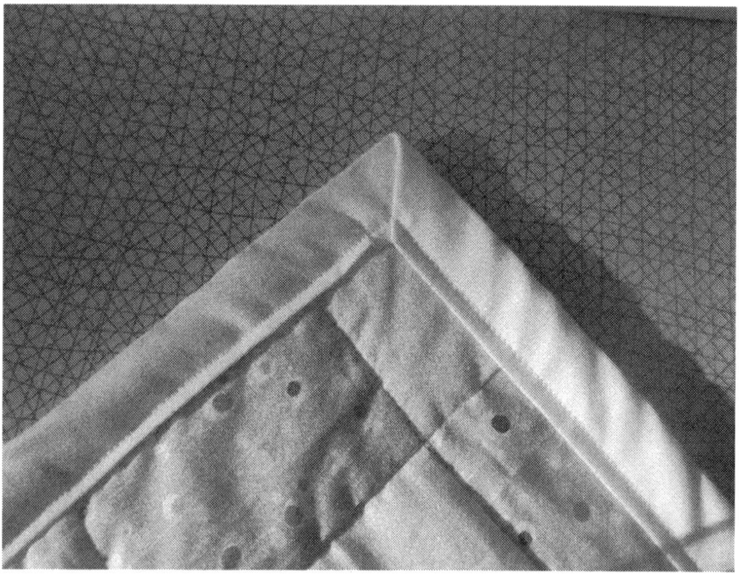

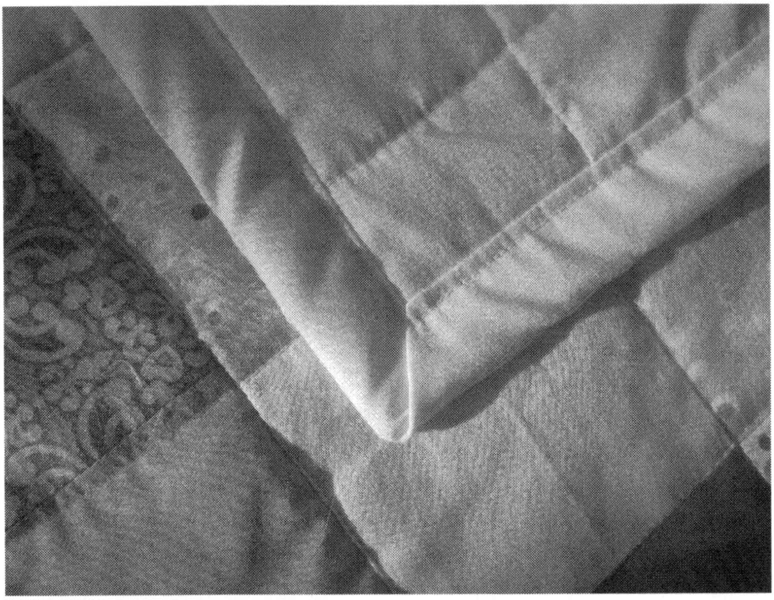

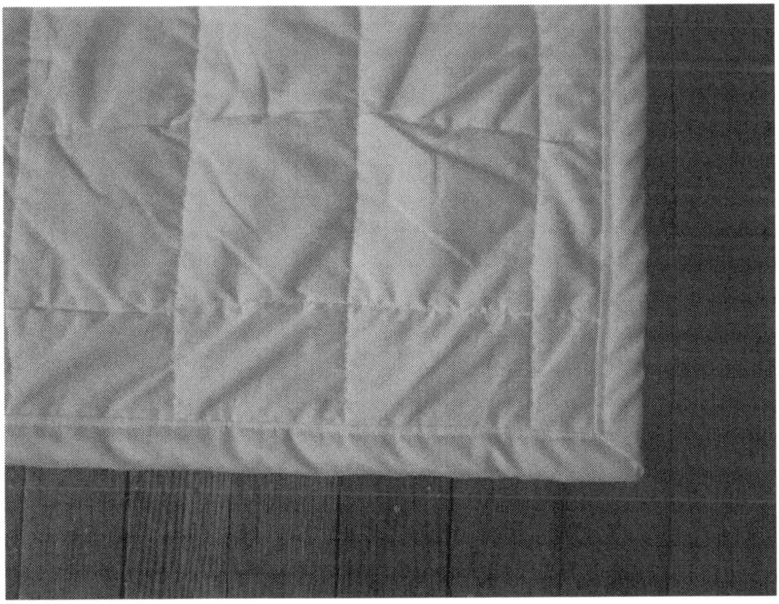

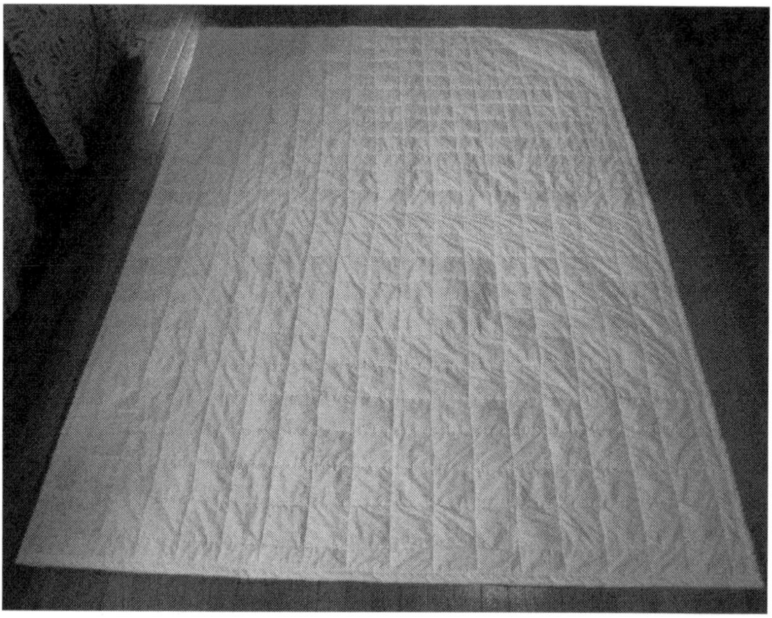

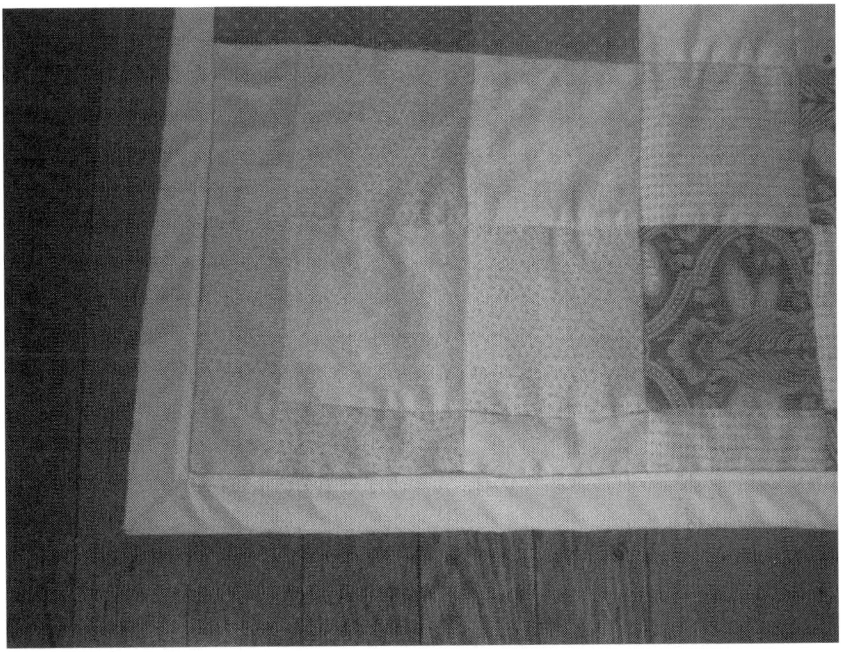

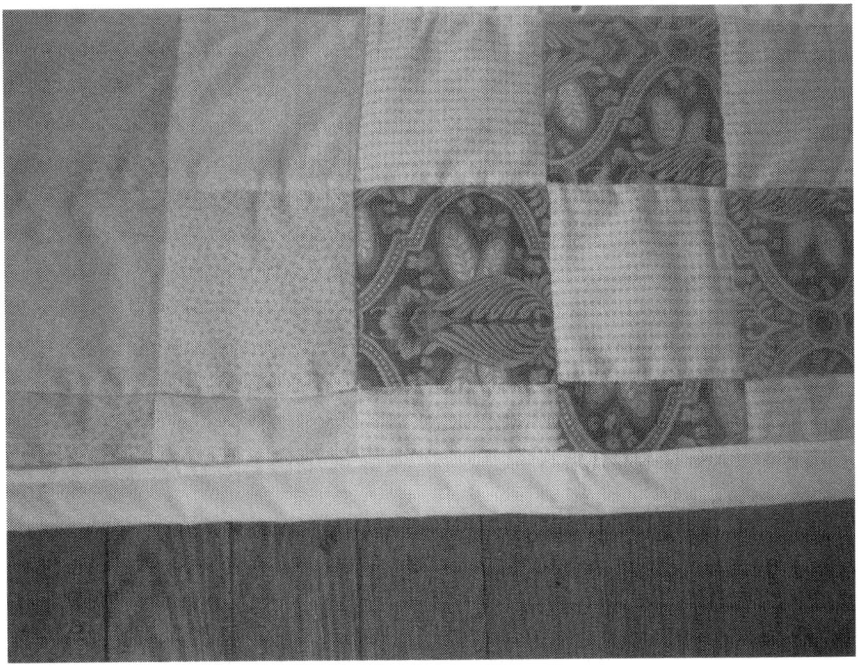

Extra photographs of the completed quilt that I did exclude from the introduction. Appreciate!

THE END

Manufactured by Amazon.ca
Bolton, ON

20911929R00081